D0179651

PENGUIN BOOKS

THE WAR AT HOME

Rachel Starnes received her MFA in Creative Nonfiction from California State University, Fresno. Her essays have appeared in *The Colorado Review* and *Front Porch Journal*. She has lived in Scotland, Texas, Saudi Arabia, Florida, California, and Nevada, and is currently on the move again with her husband, two sons, a cat, and a puppy.

Advance Praise for *The War at Home*
by Rachel Starnes

"Rachel Starnes's *The War at Home* navigates the joys, fears, compromises, and casualties that create the terrain of marriage. And if you are a military spouse, her memoir will reveal thoughts you never even knew you had. This is a wise and fearless book."

—Siobhan Fallon, author of *You Know When the Men Are Gone*

"This is one of the most honest and genuine memoirs I've ever read, as well as one of the most finely written. There's not a false note in these pages. Rachel Starnes's story is at once both singular and emblematic, and as I read it I found myself wondering just how many others out there are going through experiences similar to the author's while lacking the means to express them as she does so beautifully in this riveting account. *The War at Home* is that rare thing: a book about the here and now that promises to last well beyond next month or next year."

—Steve Yarbrough, award-winning author of
The Realm of Last Chances and *Safe From the Neighbors*

"Rachel Starnes has written elegantly and with deep feeling and insight about a common, but little written about and increasingly less understood, facet of American life. I found *The War at Home* a fascinating and compelling read."

—Karl Marlantes, *New York Times* bestselling author of
What It's Like to Go to War and *Matterhorn*

"*The War at Home* invites us into two worlds not often glimpsed—the loaded culture of Navy wives and the painful doubts of early parenting. Haunted by her troubled past, Rachel Starnes navigates these two worlds with striking honesty, exposing her faults and forging a way toward a future worth fighting for."

—Katey Schultz, award-winning author of *Flashes of War*

"*The War at Home*, Rachel Starnes's stunning literary debut, is simultaneously harrowing and heartbreaking; an unflinching portrayal of the hidden costs of military service and the everyday challenges of building a life with her Navy pilot husband. This book is a profound narrative testament to the courage required to survive the cycles of connection and disconnection that the military life demands. Starnes takes a long look at her own childhood and personal history of relationships with men who leave, and the memoir explores her struggle to avoid a similar destiny for her two young boys. Filled with poignant lines and beautifully rendered scenes, the prose is also, at times, laugh out loud funny as Starnes stumbles through temporary jobs, friendships, and homes. Through her unfailing honesty, her humor, her courage on the page, and her willingness to write into the silent spaces, the reader finds a new wartime hero in Rachel Starnes."

—Steven Church, author of *Ultrasonic: Essays* and
The Day After the Day After: My Atomic Angst

"*The War at Home* is an honest, probing self-examination of a family battling its own conflicts against the backdrop of a nation on perpetual alert."

—Alison Buckholtz, author of *Standing By:*
The Making of an American Military Family in a Time of War

"*The War at Home* instantly charmed me. The messy and realistic life of Rachel Starnes pulls back the veil on one of the most selective and specialized communities of the world—the wives of Navy TOPGUN fliers. But don't fret, there are very few finger sandwiches here—Starnes shows up to Wives Club meetings with six-packs of beer and a punk-rock attitude. With Texas wit and daughter-of-an-oil-rigger grit, she delivers a powerful memoir of military family life."

—Anthony Swofford, *New York Times* bestselling author of
Jarhead: A Marine's Chronicle of the Gulf War and Other Battles

THE
WAR AT HOME

A WIFE'S SEARCH FOR PEACE (AND OTHER MISSIONS IMPOSSIBLE)

RACHEL STARNES

PENGUIN BOOKS

PENGUIN BOOKS

An imprint of Penguin Random House LLC
375 Hudson Street
New York, New York 10014
penguin.com

An early version of Chapter 10 appeared as "Hellcat Court" in *Colorado Review*, Summer 2010.

LIBRARY OF CONGRESS CATALOGING-IN-PUBLICATION DATA

Names: Starnes, Rachel, author.
Title: The war at home : a wife's search for peace (and other missions
impossible) / Rachel Starnes.
Description: New York, New York : Penguin Books, [2016]
Identifiers: LCCN 2015038751 | ISBN 9780143108665 (pbk.)
Subjects: LCSH: Starnes, Rachel. | Navy spouses—Biography. | New
mothers—United States—Biography. | United States.
Navy—Aviation—Anecdotes.
Classification: LCC V736 .S72 2016 | DDC 359.0092—dc23

Printed in the United States of America
1 3 5 7 9 10 8 6 4 2

Set in Baskerville MT Std • Designed by Elke Sigal

Author's Note: This is a story heavily rooted in the military community, specifically the Navy's Strike Fighter Aviation community. This story is entirely true, but it is mine—narrow, imperfect, and colored by the experiences of my past—and should in no way be viewed as representative of the experiences or opinions of other military spouses. The names and identifying details of people whose lives have touched my own have been changed out of respect for their privacy.

For all of the men and women serving in our country's armed forces and for their families, whose service is no less important, I wish to convey my deepest respect and gratitude.

For my boys, O and E
And for Ross
I love you

THE
WAR AT HOME

J anuary. The sky in the dusty, drought-stricken valley of central California is a dull gray. I'm standing in the squadron hangar parking lot behind the open, empty trunk of my Honda, facing Ross. Heaped on the ground between us are various duffel bags and a backpack. I lean over for a kiss—I want just one, quick, like we talked about, no tears, no scene, just go—but he grabs my hand instead and gives me a hug that folds me into him. I resist. I can get through this, but we need to stick to the script, keep things moving.

"Be safe." These are always the first words, the ones that initiate the final good-bye checklist for any absence, short or long.

"I will," he says. "I love you." I can smell his aftershave.

"I love you too." I need these to be the magic words that will make him let go, but he holds on a few more seconds and tears fill my eyes. He will be gone six, maybe seven months, his first official deployment. I focus on the giant painted squadron logo on the side of the building, but the image wobbles and blurs. I curse myself as the rest of our good-bye turns into a fumbling negotiation of bags and straps. He walks away, heaving and juggling the weight, catches a strap in his teeth to free one hand for the door, kicks it wide with his boot, and then turns to wave. I am already buckled into the front seat and shifting into reverse. Our first official deployment, and if I could have just slowed the car to a crawl and told him to tuck and roll, I would have. I make it about a half mile down the road, just past the gate guards, before I let out the howl that's been building inside me for weeks.

Right after I dropped him off, the prospect of going back to our sparsely furnished rental and seeing everything the same but with one thing missing was so unbearable that I skipped our town completely on Highway 198 and continued on to the next town over, where, on impulse, I bought pink satin sheets. Never in my life had I been a pink satin sheet type, but now I had an excuse for stripping the blue cotton ones off the bed, the ones that held his shape from the morning and still smelled like him. New sheets would remind me that Things Were Different, so that I might avoid the awful smack of knowing after a few seconds of half-wakefulness in the morning that he was gone. They would help me avoid reaching for him, or being tricked by muscle memory into thinking he was there. No way would Ross ever get near a bed covered in pink satin.

When I finally went back to the house, I cleaned it like it was a crime scene. I found places for Ross in the backs of closets and drawers and in cabinets in the garage. I filed him away in folders and binders and a fireproof, waterproof safe. Then I threw out his favorite foods in the refrigerator.

I imagined him balking at the wastefulness of this, but what I couldn't afford was a half-used bottle of mayonnaise waiting to sabotage me for six months every time I opened the refrigerator. What I couldn't afford was a little scrap of a receipt with his crimpy handwriting popping out when I went sorting through the desk. Under no circumstances could I afford to imagine him close to me. He was allowed in picture frames. In two dimensions, under glass, and under certain circumstances, I could handle him. When I couldn't, when things felt sketchy, I needed to know where to avoid looking.

The one thing I couldn't put away was Green Jacket, which had acquired a name and a personality of its own. Ross had kept Green Jacket since the seventh grade, even after the cuffs frayed and our dog ate the hood's drawstring. Even after it got lost on a subway in Madrid, Green Jacket always made its way back to him. The simple cotton hoodie with a tiny Olympic logo on the breast was a testament to his stubbornness, to the fact that he wore T-shirts until they were frayed at the neck and threadbare. Ross loves to feel things broken in and soft. He's the only person I know who has his shoes resoled, who actually looks up cobblers in the phone book. Green Jacket I kept in reserve, tucked just under my side of the bed, for emergencies, for the nights I knew were coming, when I couldn't clean or organize anything, when every thought was steamrolled flat before it even fully formed, when the feeling of old, used up, no good crept into my skin and applied to my limbs and my bones. When I wanted to throw me out. Then I could get Green Jacket out and hold it to my face and breathe Ross in, and allow myself to think that he would always find his way home to me.

PART I

CHAPTER 1

Ross had been my younger brother Doug's best friend since sixth grade. I've always loved the semiscandalous feeling of admitting that to friends—how we transgressed the "off-limits" pact for friends of siblings. But the truth is that ours was no long-simmering, forbidden crush. We pretty much ignored each other all the way through high school, when he and Doug, smart-asses and soccer players, far surpassed me on the popularity and attractiveness scales. Ross was not so much "off-limits" as "hopelessly unattainable," and therefore an object of my derision. Those were the years when he developed the annoying habit of strolling into our house unannounced, via the door from the garage, and tossing a casual "Word up" over his shoulder at my shocked scowl.

Ross and I had actually spent a few years in junior high and high school band together before he surprised everyone and quit in his junior year. By then, I was a senior and had doubled down on my band nerd identity—sure, there was the unbearable ridiculousness of marching season, but then concert season started and we all got to sit down like actual musicians and play beautiful, complex *music*. Ross had had enough and decided to devote his time to soccer and acquiring college academic credits. To our band director's sour comment that he had his priorities all wrong, he shot back, "No, I think I've finally got them right."

I spent my Friday nights itching and sweating in my blue polyester uniform and toy soldier hat with the twelve-inch feather plume, and Ross, cut from the soccer roster just as the season began, came up with his own solution for how to spend his time by appointing himself the team's mascot. He assembled a superhero costume with a cape that read "The Guy" and ran up and down the sidelines at soccer games with a giant flag every time our side scored, much to everyone's delight.

If you'd asked me then what I thought of him, I would have said he wasn't my type, but the truth was that I didn't yet have a type. I was awkwardly tall and 1800s pale in the central Texas world of compact, athletic, sun-kissed blondes, and for the vast majority of my high school career, I didn't date. Ross's broad shoulders, piercing blue eyes, and explosion of messy brown curls meant that he had what my brother called a "case of terminal girlfriend," one long, steady, largely unremarkable relationship that lasted most of high school, which meant that he was exempt from the ongoing intrigue of high school coupling, and yet always the not-entirely-ignorant subject of several crushes. He could, and did, flirt with impunity, and for this I decided that he was dangerously full of himself.

My opinion of him remained static through our college years, when I heard that he had again acquired a long-term girlfriend at the small private liberal arts college he attended. She was beautiful, I heard, Iranian and premed, and Ross was learning phrases in Farsi, all of which made me roll my eyes and think, "Of course." I was muddling my way through a far less focused syllabus of failed relationships at the University of Texas, trying on wildly different versions of myself in the process. By the time I was two years past graduation, underemployed and single once again, I suddenly found myself face-to-face with Ross at my brother's birthday party. We were all standing outside of a Tex-Mex restaurant in Austin, waiting for a table, when Ross asked me, "So, what's going on in your life these days?"

Embarrassed, and pissed off that I was embarrassed, I answered him truthfully: "I answer phones for the college I should have left by now and I make copies for a woman who calls me 'sugar bear.' I'm also really good with a shredder. I can barely afford my rent, I think my degree may be useless, and I have no idea what I'm going to do about any of that."

"That's interesting," he said. "I'm cold-calling for an insurance salesman and living at home with my parents." He grinned. "I win." That brilliant grin, paired with the bracing shot of humility, was the thing that let me see him anew. All the old facts I knew about him—that he loved classic rock and drove a pink and white '55 Ford Fairlane that he and his dad worked on together, that he was an Eagle Scout raised in a conservative, churchgoing home but was nonetheless very convincing vamping onstage in drag with Doug for a contest in high school, that he'd earned a private pilot's license during his summers cleaning airplanes at the municipal airport and that he hoped one day to fly fighter jets for the Navy but he'd applied twice and been rejected—all these things hovered in the back of my mind. I was cynical and defensive when it came to guys, never fully convinced they weren't secretly laughing at me, but all the things I knew and remembered about Ross, along with the things I was newly discovering, turned, over the course of an evening, into the beginnings of a powerful attraction. But the biggest thing was that he kept making me laugh—actual bursts of it, not the polite snicker I generally used with guys.

Two years after college, I was still tenderly excavating myself from the wreckage of high school, and I hated the idea of parading my emotional baggage in front of someone I considered a golden boy. We exchanged phone numbers and began to e-mail each other to occupy the long hours of our soul-crushing jobs. When we started meeting up on weekends, I knew that if we continued on this path, I would have to fill him in on the convoluted story I was only just learning how to tell. Through my brother, Ross already knew the outline, but it was important that I tell it to him myself.

Back in junior high, while I was furiously practicing scales with the band, my father fell into a long period of unemployment. All my life he had worked on oil rigs, and the company he'd been with since before I was born had laid him off after a downturn in the industry. After a rough year and a half of looking for work, he found a job, only it was in Saudi Arabia, which meant uprooting our family and moving us there at the beginning of my ninth grade year. This was the story Ross knew, how his best friend moved to the Middle East for a while. What he didn't know was how that move fractured my sense of self and sent me reeling through a series of rebellions. The school on the company compound went only to ninth grade, and after completing the year in a haze of culture shock, I was shipped off at age fifteen to a boarding school. Away from the anchoring presence of my family, I sank into a deep depression, started experimenting with various drugs, and was subsequently expelled just past the midway point of my tenth grade year. I spent about six weeks in a sort of limbo, being fretted over, medicated, and shuffled between various living situations until it was arranged that an uncle on my mother's side would come and live with me in our family's mostly empty house in Texas so I could salvage the rest of the tenth grade back at Georgetown High School, where I would have ended up if we'd never moved to Saudi Arabia in the first place. My mother and brother arranged to move back to Georgetown as well, scrapping Doug's plans for some other boarding school. And there we all remained for the rest of high school, leaving my dad in Saudi Arabia until my senior year, when he finally found another job in the United States that would allow him to move back home.

Ross took all of this in with the occasional, quiet "Holy shit." He had the unnerving habit of maintaining intense eye contact while we talked, a move that made it feel like he wasn't just listening but *learning* me as he did. He could relate to some of my story—at least, more than most people I'd known in high school or college—because it turned out he'd had his own similarly timed uprooting and reshuffling away from Georgetown and back again. Ross's dad was a soil chemist who worked at several different national labs and research firms over the course of his career, and when Ross was in ninth grade, his family moved to Las Vegas, Nevada, a city he's hated ever since, and where he had to walk through metal detectors to get into school. After one year, during which he learned a mean game of pool by spending all of his free time with his dad, Ross's parents became worried about him and it was agreed that the best plan was to move him back to Georgetown, where he would live with the large and lively family of one of his friends, people he still maintains a connection to—he refers to the friend's parents as "Mom and Dad Simek." Ross's parents eventually moved back and he also finished high school in his reconstituted family. The coincidental timing of those moves gave us a lot to talk about—missing family, being the "old/new kid" in a weird living situation that required frequent explanation, feeling painfully conscious of being a logistical headache for other people, and the awkwardness of trying to reclaim old rhythms and relationships after significant interruptions.

The difference between our experiences, though, other than a whole lot of global miles, was that my passport bore the stamps from a crossover into the territory of "known fuckup" while Ross stayed firmly within the boundaries of honor student and Eagle Scout. This was important because explaining the true course of my sophomore year to someone I intended to become close to had become something of an obligatory disclaimer I had to deliver with the proper gravity—*I have the proven potential to screw up massively and be a problem and liability for everybody close to me. Do you accept the risk in investing in me?* It wasn't the kind of leverage I was fond of giving away.

By the time of our conversation at Doug's birthday party, Ross and I stood on the other side of college holding on to big dreams—his to be a fighter pilot and mine to be a writer—but grudgingly pursuing other, humbler short-term plans with no idea how or even whether the bigger stuff would work out. Soon after we began dating, Ross found a job as a billing analyst at a check printing company in San Antonio and moved into a tiny one-bedroom apartment. A hundred miles north in Austin, I left my reception job and started working as a scholarship administrator at the same university, where my desk held a framed snapshot of us tethered to climbing ropes on a cliff in Colorado, the kind of action-packed, REI catalog stunt I never would have under-taken before dating him. Our outlooks improved. We traded off cities on the weekends, and I worked hard for the approval of his dog, Abby, who started off eating my shoes and muscling me out of the bed and then grew to anticipate my hugs so much that she would rocket up the stairs to my apartment and leap into my arms.

It was on one of these afternoons, when Ross had driven up from San Antonio with Abby for the weekend and we had both finished recounting the horrors of the week in our office jobs, that Ross took a deep breath and said, "I have something I need to tell you." We were sitting on my couch and the light coming in from my small balcony was thick and golden red as the sun began to set.

"You were so honest with me about what happened with you in high school," he began, "and now I need to tell you about the worst thing that ever happened to me. Actually, it's still happening, and it will be for a long time." Then he told me that during his senior year in college, his parents broke the news that his father, at age fifty-five, had been diagnosed with a particularly virulent form of early-onset Alzheimer's disease, one that was inherited genetically.

"Before they even knew what to call the disease, my dad's family had it. We're part of some genetic study, and they've traced the roots of our particular mutation all the way back to somewhere in Russia."

He stared at the lengthening shadows on the floor and shrugged. In high school I used to think things had always come easily for Ross—good looks, popularity, a girlfriend, academic success—and now here was this grim disease that had been stalking his family for generations. Along with the terrible feeling of grief for the pain happening to someone I cared about, there was a layer of guilt for having seen him so one-dimensionally for so long.

"I feel like I'm just starting to figure out who I'm supposed to be," he said, "and I don't know how long I've got before he's gone." We talked until there was no more light in the room, our dinner plans forgotten, and at the end of the conversation I told him for the first time that I loved him.

O ur families were openly supportive of the match, which was a new thing for me—I was used to a certain lukewarm patience in my family's reactions to the boyfriends I brought home, a state we all agreed was great progress from my early college days when they often fought to conceal outright horror, sometimes at the boyfriend and sometimes at the stranger I'd become in his presence. Doug openly took credit for this fortunate turn of events, reminding me of a conversation we'd had a few weeks before his birthday party, when he'd asked me, "Why don't you date someone like *Ross*?" and my frustrated reply had been, "I don't *know* anyone like *Ross*."

So when Ross received a call from the Navy recruiter he'd been talking to with the news that he'd been accepted for OCS, Officer Candidate School, it seemed for me like the end of a lovely, unexpected dream. I knew that he had applied a third time for flight school with the Navy, but I also knew that the odds of acceptance were slim, and that he'd already been rejected without explanation twice, once at the beginning of college and once after he'd finished his degree. I admired Ross's dream to be a fighter pilot as just that—a dream—and likened it to my own of publishing a short story in *The New Yorker*. I saw us pitching to our beloved institutions every now and then, remaining largely ignored but better people for the effort. It was New Year's Eve, we had been dating for six months, and he and I were house-sitting in San Antonio for his older brother. I was sick with the flu and he was all aglow, breathlessly explaining that in another nine months, he'd be heading to Pensacola, Florida, for three months of what amounted to officers' boot camp.

"Congratulations!" I said, the word feeling like a tight, uncertain cord between us, possibly the beginning of letting him go. I got up to puke, which bought me some time to huddle quietly in the bathroom and not pelt him with questions like "But what about your life? What about your dad? *What about us?*" As he'd explained it, OCS led directly into two years of flight school, which meant relocating between several different states every eight months or so, and somewhere in there would be a point where the pilots were divvied up into their respective communities— helicopters, large reconnaissance planes, and fighters—which led to more training and eventually an assignment to a squadron in the fleet, leading to a three-year period of on-and-off deployments called the first sea tour. It all blurred together for me into an indefinite series of years in which I had no idea if I played a part. No time for "deepen your relationship and decide if you might eventually like to get married." How could we continue dating if he was always moving around? And would he honestly have any time or attention left over for me if flight school was as all-consuming as he'd made it seem? On the couch he'd seemed so lit up, so clearly excited and focused.

One thing was clear to me as I heaved and gasped in the bathroom: I wasn't ready to let him go, but he was most definitely leaving. Whatever came next wouldn't be easy. I splashed some water on my face and braced myself to be broken up with. When I came back out, he asked, "Will you come with me?"

My relief was so intense that it almost eclipsed the sudden dread and uncertainty that came with it. Nevertheless, the response came out as a question. "Yes?" I can't remember if we talked about it then, the mechanics of exactly how I was going to tag along—doing what?—living where? I do know that it was at least a week before I finally panicked, weeping into the phone one night that no, I wasn't crazy about my job, and yes, I could imagine relocating, but what if it didn't work out?

"We'll figure it out," he said, and then, as if it was the most obvious thing in the world, "We'd be married."

Oh. The actual proposal didn't take place for another five months, on the first day of May 2004, when we were sitting in the botanical garden in Fort Worth making fun of a high school senior leaning against a rock getting his picture taken in his letter jacket, his mom nearby stage-managing with a handful of outfit changes. There had been a huge thunderstorm the night before, and rose petals, millions of them, were stuck to everything, making a carefully tended garden look like it had just rolled out of bed with a hangover. The air was cold, crisp, and bright. It was beautiful. He handed me a ring and asked me to marry him.

Becoming a Navy wife wasn't something I had spent much time thinking about. Up until I met Ross, I had been fairly certain that marriage was not in my future, or if so, it was part of a distant future, like maybe after a long and tumultuous life of adventure during which I'd thoroughly established my identity and career, a formidable woman of means in my own right and not just So-and-so's wife who tags along. I'd seen enough of what work-related separations had done to my parents and I had no intention of repeating the pattern.

On top of that, we were now also talking about war, politics, oaths, service, real danger, and sacrifice. Supporting Ross in joining the Navy at a time when our country was at war in the Middle East, a place I'd briefly lived and still felt conflicted about, was a tall order. To say that I believed we were fighting for something more than oil, and that I was willing to underwrite that belief with the life of someone I loved, was something I couldn't quite do. The best I could offer was that I honored his dream to fly and that service to one's country, as a principle and as a profession, is noble. "I can live with that," he'd said. But I wasn't sure I could. Whatever the course of the war abroad, he and I would have to find some way to maintain peace at home, both in our marriage and in our chosen community. Would either place tolerate someone with as many reservations as I already had?

At its heart, the question of Ross joining the Navy brought up a feeling in me that had become distressingly familiar long before the depression, the drugs, and the expulsion from boarding school made it official: "I don't belong here." I felt it as a white, teenage American girl in Saudi Arabia, I felt it as the daughter of an oil rig worker and a public school teacher living among the rich elite in boarding school, and I felt it as the subject of unspoken scandal when I returned, medicated and disoriented, to my hometown public school. And those are just the most tangible examples—looking back, I can see the beginnings of my sense of not belonging taking root years before my family started moving around. Ross was fully committed to going somewhere I was not sure I could follow.

CHAPTER 2

My sharpest memory is a repeating one, an event that happened so many times and in so many contexts over the years that it has almost lost its meaning from wear. It looks like this: a girl, anywhere from three to seventeen years old, standing at a barrier—sometimes a rope, sometimes a gate, sometimes a giant smooth plate of glass, and sometimes nothing, just an understanding that here you can't go any farther—and watching a man, her father, most often wearing a gray windbreaker, blend into a crowd of travelers. Realist Dad becomes Pointillist Dad, and finally Impressionist Dad. Is he really: that guy in line, able to see me, waving back? He's definitely: leaving again, indistinct, already gone.

My dad's work schedule has been predictably unpredictable since before I can remember. Our kitchen calendars tracked his movements in long color-coded lines labeled with my mother's loopy, half-capitalized handwriting: "RoycE HOME!" "RoycE GonE." Shift work usually meant even measures of time on and time off—two weeks on, two weeks off, or a month on, a month off—but often there were training schools tacked on, or extended absences for towing the rig somewhere for repairs, which could mean up to three months away. Even then, weather could delay the helicopters that ferried men to and from the rig for shift change, further cheating the days home. Planning anything required a consultation with the calendar, and if the event—my piano recital, the school play, our birthdays—was too far ahead of his known schedule, the answer to questions of guest lists or permission forms was, "Just put Mom and then save a space just in case." In response to a work calendar that had no flexibility, we became fantastically rubbery in our accounting for holidays— Thanksgiving and Christmas were the only big ones we really celebrated and they slid to the left or right as needed.

I grew up as an airport regular, but one whose familiarity extended only to the gates and baggage carousels. Dropping off and picking up, two distinct routines, each with a wildly different emotional climate, took place sometimes several times a month depending on the dictates of the calendar. If his flight left early on a weekday, Doug and I would sometimes get to skip the first few hours of school. No Pledge of Allegiance, no language arts. Instead, a stick of Big Red gum shared from the pack Dad bought at the airport gift shop, its flavor pricking my tongue just like tears pricked the inside of my nose as I slouched in the backseat of the Chevrolet on the drive away from the airport. I hid the gum under my tongue when I went back to school until it was a hard, flavorless lump and then swallowed it. I didn't care if it stayed there for seven years.

It sounds horrible, but one of the things I'm grateful for about 9/11 is that people who aren't passengers can't get to the gates anymore. The gate is the worst place for saying good-bye because the difference between "here with me" and "gone somewhere else without me" is made clear and immediate. Here at the gate is the shore, but then ten feet away is the mouth of that horrible chute, that accordion-ended walkway that feeds into the plane and then hangs there open and gaping when the plane starts to taxi, looking for all the world like an amputated limb, a snipped umbilical cord, a useless and lost connection that was flimsy in the first place.

Even worse are the windows, which are so generous about giving you a full view of the plane leaving—there goes all the motion and momentum, leaving. Here you are, stuck, waiting. You are what's left behind. It's much better to part ways in a busy terminal, and I'm reminded of this small grace every time I do it. *I'm just going to walk off this way and you take your bags and go that way.* It feels more fair, if that's possible, less of a dramatic scene.

Mom and Doug and I used to stand together at the plate-glass window by the gate while Dad got on the plane, and Doug and I would press our foreheads against the cool glass and argue about which of the shoulders in the plane's tiny passenger windows belonged to Dad. I always said I could see him and that he was waving, but that was mostly to upset Doug. "You missed it! He's right there!" If I could get Doug to cry, I wouldn't have to. Then on the long walk out of the terminal, I could concentrate on stepping only in the dead center of the octagonal patterns on the airport carpet.

The "RoycE HOME" days on our kitchen calendar were underscored with a long, neat line of green highlighter and the "RoycE GonE" ones sometimes got a yellow line and sometimes just a long arrow drawn in ballpoint pen. The line system was a deceptively simple way of charting what was in fact a complicated and dramatic symphony of reactions as my dad orbited in and out of our lives, and it divided us into two very different families.

In the green line period, when we were at "RoycE HOME," an initial recovery period would give way to days that felt even and good. Green line periods started with picking Dad up at the airport, where he would hug us so hard our backs would pop. Doug and I would chase his bags around the luggage carousel and argue over who got to wrestle them out into the parking lot, our faces pressed into the green canvas, which still smelled of fuel and smoke, with our last name written in Sharpie ink in big, block letters. Then we'd get back to the house and he'd collapse face-down on the bed for an indeterminate amount of time, during which the only important thing was to BE QUIET. When he was home and fully recovered, Dad gave "bed throws," hurling us bodily again and again into the mattress of his and Mom's king-sized bed, letting us shriek with laughter as we barely missed the blades of the ceiling fan. He would play catch with us in the front yard and teach us how to field grounders, and we would pitch him tennis balls just to see him smash them with our tiny aluminum bat, the ball flying far over our house and into the next block. When he was home, Dad would go on long runs in the morning and come back just when we were getting up to eat breakfast; covered in sweat and radiating energy, he'd teasingly menace us with a big, wet hug.

He was a giant to me, with thick shoulders and a broad back so hard that when I hung on to his shoulders at the local swimming pool, it seemed like some force of nature was parting the waters with a speed that was almost scary, like I wasn't sure I could hang on. I had the perfect vantage point from which to rub sunscreen on his bald spot, round and centered like Friar Tuck's, and being allowed this intimacy—Dad wasn't a fan of the bald spot, or the necessity of protecting it—always thrilled me, like I finally had a way of caring for him. He had little freckles there, just like the ones on my face.

When he was home, Dad rarely talked about work. I knew the names of the various jobs he'd occupied—roustabout, rough-neck, assistant driller, driller, tool pusher, foreman—and that the flights we saw him board took him to a port city where he then caught a helicopter out to wherever the rig was, but my imagination stopped there. Thus it was always a complete mystery and a huge disappointment when it turned out every time that he was actually going back again. I remember clearly when Doug and I finally lit upon the solution of hiding Dad in the closet when it was time for him to go back. "We won't tell anyone," we promised, "and if they come to the door we'll say you're not here." Dad laughed, and we got indignant, reassuring him that of course we'd bring him food and let him out only when it was safe, but when it became clear that he wasn't even seriously considering the option, we both got even more confused. Didn't he want to stay?

The days leading up to his departure were a weird sine wave of affection on my parents' part that peaked early and then took a dive toward aggression as they prepared themselves for separation by picking an old scab of a fight. It was usually some variation on the theme of "What do you care how [xyz] works out? You'll be gone," and "How the hell do you think this family got a roof over its head?" that made for a full day of yelling, complete with the requisite hurled dish on Mom's part and squealing tires on Dad's. At times like this they were strangers to us, huge and loud, distorted, two forces bent on collision.

Somehow they'd make up behind their closed bedroom door the night before he left, or if that hadn't worked, some uneasy pause in the battle would prevail on the way to the airport. But always, by the time we got to the gate, the good-byes were long and passionate, full of embraces where they said quiet, muffled things into each other's necks.

When we were younger, Doug and I would cry and try to squirm our way into this last hug, but as I got older I began to realize that the other passengers and the airline attendants were watching us. This might be a false memory, but I recall a stewardess leaning down and saying something syrupy to me like, "Aw, you're gonna miss your dad, aren't you?" prompting the sudden realization that we were doing this *publicly*, that my family was this big oozing ball of emotion in the middle of a busy airport. Nobody else ever seemed to have a problem getting on a plane, and I never remember seeing anyone else crying.

As a kid, I think this sudden recognition of exposure offended me because my dad's leaving was a wound every time he did it, and I felt that there was a real chance that if he finally saw how much it hurt us he would find a way to stop doing it. So much seemed to hang in the balance, so why did strangers have to look at me while I was hurting like this? Now I look back at this sobbing family at the American Airlines gate and think, We did this *all the time*. My God, it's even likely the same stewardesses saw us every time, maybe even watched me grow up over the years. I wonder what it looked like, the process by which I got quieter and angrier as the years passed in the hallways of Robert Mueller Municipal Airport.

Once he was gone it was like the three of us let go of a collectively held breath. We could now begin the switch over to "RoycE

GonE," the three-pronged family unit that operated under completely different rules. McDonald's was a given for the first meal, and all that heat and salt and sugar sat in my stomach like a benediction made even better by the fact that we could eat in the car, or at a park—anywhere so that we didn't have to arrange ourselves around an empty seat at the kitchen table. The first few Dad-less days were like a long slumber party with Mom, and I bathed in the floodlight of her attention and took advantage of the relaxed rules of the parent/kid hierarchy. I campaigned to stay up late and watch *Dallas* or *Moonlighting* with her, to take tiny sips of her beer, and to lean my shower-wet head back against her knees after she combed the tangles out. I told myself I was more like a companion now, a good friend she could rely upon to help out around the house and to keep Doug, though only a year younger than me, in check, since he was still a kid and couldn't be expected to be reasonable or mature.

Mom pep-talked us through errands and chores and minor emergencies in this first stage with assurances that "this will be an adventure we can tell Dad about." A phone call from him when he was gone was rare and a big deal, and since phone time was limited, the pressure to come up with a pithy and compact report on my days since we'd last spoken was a challenge to which I responded by living each moment with an eye toward editing and retelling the experience to my dad, deciding whether whole days made the cut or not. On longer hauls, I remember sending him elaborate drawings and a long, rather forced poem about my doomed attempt at pitching on my softball team.

Early into one of Dad's absences, our collective mood was cheerful, a can-do attitude in the face of an expected hardship that would just require a little ingenuity and creativity. Cautiously optimistic, I kept up my own interior monologue during this period, telling myself, "With a little planning, this can be way better than last time," and "Just pay attention and don't screw up." What's remarkable about being a kid is that, through force of will, your faith in illusions can last far longer than it should. I told myself these things every time, and every time I believed them as we moved right into the next inevitable stage of "RoycE GonE," the Total Meltdown.

I could feel a Total Meltdown coming the way I imagine some people claim they feel storms coming by a pain in an old knee injury. It was a kind of low emotional barometric pressure that I could sense just in the slack way Mom would put down a breakfast plate or the way she would rake one hand through her curls to push them out of her eyes. At times like this, her eyes would elude me when I tried to catch her attention with a funny face or tell her a joke that went on a little too long because I was already getting nervous and forgetting the ending. All my energy went into strategies of distraction for her, and I kept up a constant scan of the house to catch things that might piss her off—a messy pile of clothes I could kick into my closet, dishes in the sink, a microwave popcorn bag left out by the TV. Doug must have sensed something too, because it was always these times when he pushed back at the rules or he broke something with what seemed to me like obvious intent. I harried him and picked at him and threatened him, convinced that he was the errant spark that would start the blaze. And then somehow it always happened. One little thing—a spilled mug of hot chocolate is one I remember clearly, but it seems like spills of any kind always did this to us—would suddenly become a very big thing, and all three of us would be sucked into a fast spiral.

"God damn it!" Mom's opening volley.

"I'm sorry! I'm sorry!" Whichever kid is at fault.

"Get a towel!" An increase in volume, panic circuits lighting up all around.

"Don't yell!" Yelled, of course.

"Shit! It's getting everywhere!" Time is now a factor, messes are spreading, and the towel is inadequate.

"I'm sorry!" Default response, also inadequate, tick-tock, tick-tock.

"Hurry up!" Whichever kid is not at fault joining the game.

"Quit YELLING!" Screamed, this time.

"SHUT UP! *YOU* QUIT!" The other kid, in a desperate, failed bid to curry favor with Mom or else short-circuit the reaction.

"Fuck you!" Both kids facing off against each other, easier opponents and more familiar rivals in these meltdown moments.

"Watch your mouths!" Mom reasserting herself, now with both a mess and a fight to contain.

"Fuck *you!*" The other kid, not to be outdone, gets out the big gun in the sibling standoff. Complete anarchy ensues, physical combat between the kids if they're within each other's reach; otherwise, engagement of projectiles. An ultimate explosion is needed.

"Fuck *all* of this! I'm so sick of this! *I want out of this marriage!*" Mom delivers the cannon shot that scatters all combatants, and like some triggered land mine we would all go flying apart in a roar of profanity and tears and slamming doors, a sad, half-cleaned mess the only marker of the conflict left behind.

The resulting sulk would be long and quiet and sour and I was often the last to come out of it, feeling doubly wronged because I was so convinced that I was the only one who had worked to try to prevent the whole thing. My consolation in these sulks was a promise I made to myself, written over and over again on the pink pages of a diary otherwise given over to fantasies and doodles: "I will never, ever do this to myself or my kids. I will never, ever marry a man who leaves." As I got older and meaner, I started throwing this little barb out at my mom when she would try to break the ice and apologize.

The hot chocolate incident is my clearest memory of the sudden appearance of the nuclear specter of divorce, which in itself was a tricky concept because it seemed so common in the lives of my friends at school, and because many of my schoolmates assumed that my dad's infrequent presence meant my parents were already divorced. But I lived in fear of the idea, enthralled by it, the way standing near a huge drop-off can make you feel like you're actually leaning into it. Just as I believed every time that my dad might change his mind and not leave for work, or that I could short out the circuit that led to our family explosions when he was gone, I believed that every time they invoked the word "divorce," the event was imminent. It was Doug who finally whispered to me from the backseat of our car, still rocking from where Dad had slammed the passenger's side door and begun his long walk back home from a rare family dinner out, "Maybe we'd be better off if they did."

What I wish my parents had said to me during those moments when it seemed everything would explode, that separation, abandonment, and chaos were imminent: "This threat isn't real. It will pass." What I'm terrified that I can't say, even now, to my own children: "I have no idea if the threat is real or not. We're making it up as we go along."

CHAPTER 3

We love you, Pensacola, YOU ARE BEAUTIFUL!"

"NO LOOTERS. This property is armed."

"Why, Ivan?"

"State Farm is a lying neighbor who cheats and STEALS from you!!!"

When I arrived in Pensacola, Florida, as a newlywed, forty-eight hours married and in the front seat of a U-Haul with the dog in my lap, the city was still reeling from the damage from Hurricane Ivan, which had stomped it flat only two months prior, while Ross was finishing Officer Candidate School. Spray-painted messages that ranged from mournful to outright profane decorated the fronts of storm-gutted homes and businesses. Ross and his classmates had sheltered beneath desks in a cryptology bunker, later emerging to distribute MREs to newly homeless civilians and clean up fire ant–covered debris, their OCS syllabus on indefinite hold, while I had busily continued planning our wedding in Austin on the weak promise that he would probably be there.

My mom, laughing, had proposed a contingency plan to avoid thousands of dollars in cancellation fees by exchanging vows at the altar with Ross represented via cell phone (and following up later with a justice of the peace if cell phone unions weren't considered legal), but I'd been unable to either join her in laughing or come up with a suitable counterproposal. Instead, I'd found myself in the minor emergency clinic with what I believed to be totally unrelated chest pains, and when basic tests turned up nothing, I'd surprised both the doctor and myself by bursting into hiccuping tears when she asked, "Is there any kind of unusual stress in your life right now?" In the end, Ross made it, and the evening was one of those magical ones where time and its passing seem so utterly beside the point that I actually stopped to notice things like the smell of fresh rosemary in the table centerpieces and the crisp precision of Ross's freshly cut hairline before his Florida tan began on its way down to the stiff white color of his uniform coat. But military life had stepped in quick on the heels of our Friday night vows, and by Sunday morning, we were packed and on the road to Pensacola.

Navigating a new city is difficult in ordinary circumstances. The fallout from a major hurricane added in a new set of obstacles—street signs had blown away, and many of the major landmarks locals would have used to guide a stranger were destroyed, disguised, or displaced. Sailboats from the harbor had ended up wedged on top of park benches downtown; whole cliffsides had eroded, taking homes with them; blue plastic tarps covered nearly every roof in town; and the baseball field near our condo breathed clouds of steam in the mornings from giant mountains of mulch that arrived by the dump truck load, all that remained of Pensacola's fallen trees.

It was like everyone was lost, but calling myself "lost" at any given moment felt like co-opting a sensitive word. In admitting I was new to the city, I was also admitting that I hadn't lost anything in the hurricane. My sense of "home" was in flux, but not for the same reasons as the people around me. My landmarks—my maiden name, my job, my friends, having my family nearby, a familiar city and state—were gone, and the loss of them felt profound and disorienting, but not in a way that I felt I had any right to claim. After all, I was a newlywed. I was supposed to be feeling giddy, besotted love and a sense of rightness, the kind of joy that makes you practice writing your new signature over and over and contentedly start feathering a nest. Instead, I found myself devoting whole mornings to sitting, shivering, on Pensacola Beach and watching dump trucks bring load after load of the cold, powder-soft winter sand to a giant conveyor belt to sift out all the forks and picture frames and bicycle tires and chunks of asphalt.

For Ross, the construction of his new life as an Ensign hit snags and delays of its own. As I browsed want ads and planned open-ended tours of the rubble-strewn city, he dressed in his crisp khaki uniform, pinned on his "butter bars" and nameplate, and reported to the base to be told, each morning for the next six months, that his Ground School class was delayed, but to report back bright and early the next morning in case they needed him for random administrative chores. I could tell being "stashed" was driving him slowly nuts, that the wire-edged alertness left over from OCS was dulling, and that my continued bouts of diffuse sadness were utterly perplexing to him, but I was of little help in any of this. I got a job at a bookstore sorting through storm-damaged inventory and spent an unhealthy amount of time baking batch after batch of cookies to compensate for my lack of skill in cooking anything else, battling a continual string of sinus infections from the pink, foamy mold that grew in the storm-damaged walls of our tiny apartment, and reading depressing Russian novels.

When the action of flight school finally kicked back in for Ross, it did so with a vengeance. Over the course of the next two years, he traveled all over the country and was dunked, dragged, thrown, and spun through a variety of training experiences meant to prepare him for the physical rigors of flight, all while cramming volumes of text into his head so that he could be ready at a moment's notice to repeat, verbatim, any number of restrictions, warnings, parameters, and procedures.

In Florida, they strapped him into a helicopter cabin rigged on a giant rotating hoist above a swimming pool, and then sent the cabin hurtling down fifteen feet into the water, where it flipped upside down—*Wait for the cabin to settle and then—quick!—unbuckle yourself, find the nearest exit in the dark, and wait your turn among your cabinmates to swim out the window and follow the bubbles up, up!*

In Alabama, "redneck parasailing": With an open parachute strapped to his back and a harness running from his chest to the back end of a pickup truck eighty yards away, Ross waited for a man with a megaphone to yell, *Run!* He ran and the truck drove faster and faster until the parachute billowed and Ross's feet left the ground and he floated up and up and up, and then the truck slowed down and he floated back to earth, the idea now to hit the ground in what's called a PLF (parachute landing fall), which is like a controlled body crash, and to unclip from the chute before it dragged him to death. They did this just over the border in Alabama since it was illegal in Florida.

Back in Florida, a rigid-hulled inflatable boat dumped him out in Pensacola Bay in his flight gear, where he treaded water for a half hour before a helicopter showed up and squatted over him, blasting rotor wash and noise and dangling a cable connected to a hoist—*Grab it! Clip in! Cross your ankles!* Also in Pensacola, he sat with a line of guys in a pressure chamber and performed simple calculations as someone drained the oxygen out of the room—*Play patty-cake now with the guy across from you! See? You can't do it! Feel that euphoria? Feels like you're okay, doesn't it? But look at yourselves—this is hypoxia!*

In California, he climbed into a centrifuge—a huge salad spinner—and strapped himself into a harnessed seat in front of a camera. An engine spooled up and he spun around the room on the end of a giant counterweight until the centrifugal force reached approximately seven and a half g's and he began to get tunnel vision, at which point someone watching him on a screen alerted someone else and the voice, always the voice, yelled over a loudspeaker, *Squeeze! Squeeze your legs and your ass!*

I made myself useful during this period by helping him memorize flight maneuvers, aircraft and engine limitations, and emergency procedures verbatim for his flight briefs. The numbers and acronyms were interesting and completely foreign, a chant that made little sense but was soothing in repetition. I would quiz him while he showered and I wiped the steam from the mirror to put on mascara. "Out-of-control-flight procedure? Engine fire warning light? Emergency exit?"

Through the hiss of the water he would splutter back his answers in a rapid stream of words. "Canopy: open. Harness: release. Parachute: unfasten, evacuate aircraft. *Warning!* If aircraft is evacuated on ground while wearing parachute with lanyard connected, parachute will deploy, possibly inflating and dragging pilot in windy conditions; in a postcrash fire, pilot will be dragged into fireball." Sometimes he would do it in a singsong voice, confident in his mastery.

"It's '*should postcrash fire occur*, pilot *could* be dragged into fireball,' " I corrected. Over and over, the tiny pilot in my mind asphyxiated when his oxygen system failed, lost track of his altitude in an uncontrolled spin, and blinked in panic, as I would, at any number of sudden warning lights. The words of the procedures were an incantation against accident, and our exchange of them a contract—I'll support you in this, and you'll come back to me safely. It was terrifying and comforting, and I insisted on absolute accuracy.

And all that time, there were others to outperform, slots to compete for in the great siphoning off of student pilots coming into the pipeline of helicopters, electronic surveillance planes, and fighter jets. Ross wanted fighters, the F/A-18 Super Hornet specifically, and he explained to me his estimation of the costs and benefits of each community. "Community," in this case, meant the group of pilots flying a particular aircraft, not a fixed location in the country, since each aircraft had a series of home bases through which its pilots could potentially rotate over the course of a career. It was an interesting trick of semantics—co-opting a word for "home" and replacing it with a military aircraft. The "Hornet community," he allowed, could move us to some pretty underwhelming physical locations—tiny towns either in south Texas or Mississippi for training, and then one of two places to prepare to join the fleet: Lemoore, a small town in California's Central Valley near Fresno, or the place most people hoped for, and the only large city on the menu, Virginia Beach, Virginia. The jet community would also be more competitive and stressful in comparison to others, but that was hardly surprising for a hypermacho group that sometimes differentiated itself by calling its members "carnivores" and everyone else "herbivores." In Ross's estimation, this was exactly where he wanted to be.

The weeks before he was assigned a community were some of the most stressful for the two of us. I saw the crossover into Hornet territory as a concrete step toward war, and a level of active participation in it that terrified me both for the danger and separations it involved and for the possibility that Ross might one day be responsible for taking lives. Ross didn't see it that way. He was getting closer to a dream he'd been working hard for, one that would ask for great sacrifices but would offer the chance at being the best at something. As for the question of taking lives, he said, "I could be the guy protecting Marines on the ground who call in air support. I could be saving lives too."

When the selections came out and he got jets, he was so clearly happy that he seemed to vibrate with it, but he was almost superstitiously quiet too. When we met up for drinks with his friends from flight school, many of whom were still reeling, either happily or gloomily, about their own fates, Ross said little about the future and instead directed his conversation to the hilarity and shared trials of the past. He knew something I didn't know fully. This was good-bye; we would never see many of these people again.

Things would change between the two of us as well. I had helped Ross memorize data and procedures for the small trainer propeller plane everyone flew in the beginning of flight school, and then in his first trainer jet, and that little bit of shared effort had made me feel like I had a small but important role to play. But when Ross moved on to the F/A-18 Super Hornet, his training manuals were classified and locked in a vault, where he had to check in with an intelligence specialist, leave his cell phone outside, and keep his written notes in a binder that stayed in the vault. I was shocked to discover how keenly I missed our repetitive study sessions, and how much it felt like a door had been closed in our relationship and what we could share of this job that affected the both of us so profoundly.

Finding an identity for myself during flight school was like trying to plant a garden in a highway median. Every time I landed a job and built up some relationships in it, another relocation order would come plowing through it. After the retail bookstore job in Pensacola, I found a part-time job teaching community college writing labs in Corpus Christi, Texas, while Ross worked his way up to the selection to jets, and I held on to that job tenaciously when we moved an hour south, to Kingsville. Between the commute and my limited hours, I barely broke even on the endeavor, but it was hard enough to convince someone to hire a military spouse who would definitely relocate. Also, it felt vital to hold on to something of my own, some reason, no matter how tiny, for me to be in a particular location beyond just following Ross.

Once, in Corpus Christi, I showed up at a gathering of Navy spouses that had been mentioned in an e-mail chain I'd received. I was there for a half hour, fielding a flurry of polite but obviously confused questions about where I had come from, before someone finally said, loudly, "*Oh*, you're a *student's* wife!" The unspoken understanding, at least for this place—which was patiently and politely explained to me as I stood there trying not to let the drink in my hand shake with my humiliation—was that so many students came through the class, and stayed so briefly even if they didn't wash out and get eliminated from the pilot program, that, though the e-mail list included everyone, the wives' club was really open to only the instructors' wives.

I had a friend, Annie, who taught labs alongside me at the community college in Corpus Christi and was married to her college sweetheart, another student pilot. She and I got along well and it saddened me when she quit the job to have a baby and move with her husband to Kingsville, where he had been assigned to the E-2 pipeline, command and control planes. When Ross selected for jets, the silver lining for me was that we'd be moving to Annie's town, since both the jet and the E-2 communities trained there. It was a few months after she'd had her baby when she invited me to start attending the weekly brunch of a few of the other wives she was getting to know in the E-2 community, and I jumped at the chance to reconnect.

"I don't think they'll mind, even though you're a jet wife," she said jokingly.

"Yeah, well, I didn't marry the plane," I replied. But Annie's veiled warning turned out to be true. It *did* matter that I wasn't one of them. They would all be cycling through the same set of cities in the future, their husbands all on a timeline that meant they would be hitting career landmarks simultaneously. It seemed obvious to me that Annie and I really had more in common as friends than she did with the other E-2 wives, one of whom was downright nasty to her, but what I was learning was that our friendship had an expiration date that was rapidly approaching. She and I might never see each other again, but she would need to find a way to make peace with the other women for years.

Career talk wasn't the only subject that seemed to bring up an invisible wall between the brunch wives and myself. Though they were all at least five years younger than me—I was twenty-seven at this point and two years married—three out of four of them had children. The hard part was that I wanted very much to have a baby, but I couldn't imagine how we would manage it with our current lifestyle, and this actually had less to do with Ross's job and more to do with my own stalled career goals. Some kind of advanced degree, I had decided, would be my way of shoring up a credential before I took the plunge into motherhood, but that would require us to stay in one place long enough for me to get it. Until then, I sat glumly stuffing quiche into my mouth, listening to the impossible challenges of chafed nipples and episiotomy stitches, and realizing I had nothing appropriate to say. The extra years I had on these women had been spent answering phones for a living, dating without any sense of purpose, and getting blackout drunk on the weekends. I hadn't planned for this life. Ross and I seemed to occupy this weird middle ground between the single pilots we knew who were dating and partying and the married ones with babies and full sets of matching furniture. We had a foot in both worlds, but belonged wholly to neither.

When I finally found my own sort of community, it was in the wives' club in Kingsville, Texas, while Ross was going through the advanced syllabus in flight school. The Lady Redhawks were exactly the type of group I never would have joined if I hadn't married Ross. I didn't consider myself a "club person" even for my own passions, and couldn't imagine becoming one for a group that existed because all of its members' husbands worked together. Nevertheless, the Lady Redhawks surprised me. Even going to the first meeting took lots of psyching up. I made Ross double-check with his instructors that I was welcome before I risked another humiliation.

What made the Lady Redhawks different as a group started with its leadership—the commanding officer's wife, Mariah, was a jeans and beer woman who took the unorthodox approach of encouraging the group to elect a president and a vice president, and a whole board, and then treat her as its very laid-back trustee, as opposed to the more common model of taking on the presidential role, and all the activity planning, herself. The result was a blurring of the lines of rank and seniority among all of us, a more relaxed atmosphere in which it was actually possible to let go, for a moment, of the awkwardness of hanging out with someone whose husband was helping decide the fate of my own. By far, though, the most helpful part about the wives' club I belonged to in Kingsville was Lady Redhawk Day, an interactive tour of the flight simulators, radar room, control tower, and paraloft for which we were encouraged to borrow one of our husbands' flight suits. The finale was getting to strap on a helmet, mask, and ejection seat harness and take a brief but thrilling full-speed trip down the runway in the backseat of a trainer jet before the pilot, a very patient instructor who coached us on a few radio calls and warned us to keep our hands off the ejection handle, taxied back to the hangar to pick up yet another wife. Mariah encouraged us all to attend by warning us, "You'll never get another opportunity with the Navy like this again."

Throughout Ross's three-year tenure in flight school, this was one of two official indications I had that the Navy knew I existed. The other was a brief form he brought home just after we first arrived in Kingsville. Where could I be located in the event there was an "incident" on the flight line? The form suggested: "Bridge club, dancing, other service clubs?" Did I have any medical conditions that might make hearing unpleasant news particularly dangerous? Would I like a clergyman present when they notified me? In Kingsville with the Lady Redhawks, I learned to appreciate the comfort of camaraderie with the other women who'd had to fill out such a form, even when it was clear we had very little else in common.

B y the time Ross earned his wings and we were ready to leave Kingsville and flight school behind, I was sad to see it go. I'd managed to make a few more friends and my job was ready to promote me, plus it had been nice being a mere four-hour drive from my family in central Texas. I had hoped for us to be assigned to Virginia Beach, Virginia, next, a city big enough to have a few universities within striking distance, and a variety of programs I had been researching—teaching, writing, maybe American literature, maybe even something like history or Middle Eastern studies. There were summer workshops, museums, art festivals—many more places I felt I had a likelihood of finally finding a niche, a purpose. We listed Virginia Beach as our first choice and crossed our fingers, but then the orders came through: Lemoore, California. The next stage was a stint in the FRS, or Fleet Replacement Squadron, which everyone still called by its old acronym, the RAG, or Replacement Air Group, a giant training squadron to teach the newly minted pilots to fly the F/A-18 Super Hornet. After Ross completed his time in the RAG, there would be another opportunity to try for Virginia Beach, for the next three-year stage in his career. Maybe grad school could wait until then. After three relocations in three years of flight school, I was confident I could do anything for twelve months.

Also tempering my disappointment was the thought that

moving to California at least meant Ross would go to SERE school—Survival, Evasion, Resistance, and Escape—at Warner Springs near San Diego. Ross had already set his sights on this next hurdle, a grim crash course in what to expect as a downed pilot in hostile territory. If he was going to be stranded in the woods without food or water for a week, and then hunted, captured, and subjected to the kind of treatment that required a psychological out-processing evaluation afterward, at least at the Warner Springs location he might have a chance of staying warm. The other SERE location was in Maine.

And so again, the movers came and packed up our modest collection of inherited furniture into one third of an eighteen-wheeler headed east to pack in two other military families on the move. We loaded up our vehicles with dishes, towels, computers, clothes, toiletries, flight gear, medical records, PowerBars, audiobooks, walkie-talkies to scout for cheap gas, and our dog-eared *National Geographic Road Atlas*. The cat rode with me, the dog rode with Ross, and we set out for a 1,700-mile trek to our next destination—a town, but no address, since we intended to find someplace to rent once we got there. This is the way to move when you've got no real foothold in the world beyond a few thousand pounds of household goods. It allows for speed and a certain sense of adventure, the kind that makes you turn the radio up and sing, even in a sudden spring hailstorm that spooks even the truckers, who pull off at the rest stops while the sky turns green and ice sludges up in ridges on the road. You keep going at full speed and full volume, because this makes the trip strenuous enough to avoid any thoughts about what might be waiting at the end.

CHAPTER 4

SERE school became a part of the military's training curriculum for aircrew and special operations personnel, who are seen as having the highest risk of enemy capture, after the Korean War, and its coverage of resistance techniques was expanded to address lessons learned from prisoners of war in Vietnam. "The mission of SERE is to ensure those Americans fighting in the Armed Forces of our country, defending our freedoms and way of life, are armed with the confidence, knowledge, and skills required to survive the challenges of isolation in hostile environments." This is how FASOTRAGRUPAC (Fleet Aviation Specialized Operational Training Group, Pacific—the Navy loves acronyms, even five-syllable ones) explains why, after a few days of reviewing edible plants and principles of concealment in a classroom in San Diego, it takes people northeast into the mountains and re-creates the experience of being stranded, hunted, captured, and interrogated in hostile territory. The SERE school headquarters at Naval Air Station North Island says it more clearly in big bold letters on the front of its building. "We train the best for the worst."

"The worst," of course, even in simulation, is a matter of wild speculation. Graduates of SERE are sternly warned not to talk about what they've been through, and most would rather not anyway. The few we met before moving to California gave us a wide-eyed, ghoulish laugh when Ross or I asked what it was like, what to expect. "It fucking sucks! But at least you'll lose weight!" was the usual response.

Within forty-eight hours of our arrival in California, Ross left with a shaving kit and little else. An ominous directive indicated that he needed to bring only flight boots, that his SERE instructors would provide the rest. The boots, of course, had been accidentally packed in with the household move, and their absence provided another opportunity to feel like I had somehow screwed up what little my end of the bargain required of me and was sending him off woefully unprepared. We said good-bye on the front porch and I promised to find his boots and FedEx them when our stuff arrived. With any luck, they might catch up to him before the classroom portion of SERE ended and the wilderness simulation began.

"See you in two weeks," he said.

"Be safe," I said, our now familiar incantation. "I love you."

For the first week that Ross was gone, I struggled to pass the time, since it would be another ten days before the moving truck arrived. We'd made it to California in three days and found a house to rent as soon as we hit town, in the hour before the real estate office closed. We were in such a rush to claim an address—

road weary, short on cash, mercilessly crossing off items on the to-do list—that we ended up in our empty house with no refrigerator. We only discovered this standing in the kitchen with a six-pack of beer and a pizza in our hands, prepared to eat and then fall asleep on the living room floor with towels rolled up under our heads for pillows.

"God damn it," Ross said. "Another thing to do." We laughed and ate our dinner, then curled up together on the floor, listening to the click of our dog's toenails on the floors as she paced in the dark, new space. We had time to get a refrigerator and an air mattress before Ross left for SERE school. After that, I spent the time wandering the town on foot with Abby. My goal was to avoid racking up any more expenses on the already strained credit card and to wear myself out enough to sleep at night instead of lying awake worrying—about money, about where the hell I was going to work, about the blurriness of our future at the end of the year, but mostly about Ross. The truth was that we'd spent the last three years at such a hectic pace that I felt like I hadn't gotten a chance to really get to know him. There had been no honeymoon, and the nights spent cramming for tests, simulations, and flights left little room for anything else. One of the first things my brother had told me when I told him Ross and I were dating was, "You know, he's a really private guy. Don't take it personally." By now, I knew what he meant. I knew just enough of Ross to understand that behind the joker and the performer were vast stretches of territory that were inaccessible to most people. He was like a national park that wasn't built for tourists—a great visitors' center, but then no roads, very few paths, and a breathtaking wilderness I'd only begun to explore. I hated taking the risk that he might not be the same when he came back, that I might not even know what had changed or been broken, and that I had no clue how to handle any of it. The empty house, the empty days before my mother came out to help, and then the mover showed up, gave me plenty of room to really *think* about what we were doing, and for the first time in three years I had the time to get really, really scared.

He came back fifteen pounds lighter. He came back with hollowed-out cheeks and greenish shadows on the skin around his eyes. He came back with two long yellow-green bruises running over the tops of his shoulders and down his chest, like suspenders.

"What is this from?" I asked, putting my hands lightly on either side of his chest when he took his shirt off for bed, and slowly images formed in my head. I could feel his ribs moving beneath my palms, too close to the surface. There's a word for this, and we're not allowed to say it. Its definition was still months from being officially debated on the Senate floor after the release of the Senate Intelligence Committee's report on CIA interrogation techniques. Suddenly I took my hands away. I didn't want this in my head. I didn't want the sound of him gasping for breath or choking, even if the experience was for his own good, even if it was meant to prepare him and help him fight back.

"I can't tell you." It's a guilty feeling, this thing that sits between us when he's had to say that. How do I support him when I don't know what's happening to him? Over the years I have come to understand and accept that this is Ross's dream, but there have been times when I have wondered if there is such a thing as a dream that costs too much. There is a line we have approached, that night after SERE school and several times since, where I search my heart and know that my desire to understand Ross's experience in the Navy only goes so far. I'm not sure I can keep doing this—starting over, going it alone for long stretches, missing him, worrying about him, signing our lives over to a largely mute and incomprehensible bureaucracy—if I know about every single cost exacted along the way. When I'm feeling generous, I call my hanging back behind this line "practicality." In my darker moments, I call it by other names: "weakness," "willful ignorance," and "dereliction of duty." If loving someone is knowing them, knowing all of them and accepting them for who they are, then perhaps my love is imperfect, lacking. Perhaps I am a coward.

Early the next evening I started to drive Ross to nearby Fresno for a nice dinner, a forty-five-minute drive through flat, open cotton fields and raisin vineyards. He was quiet and kept fidgeting with the radio, loud music, different music, no music, he couldn't decide. I noticed that he was digging his fingers into the edges of the seat and clenching his mouth.

"What's the matter?"

"Nothing, I just . . . it's all so open out here. There's so much space."

I saw, suddenly, the lazy open blue of the sky and straight lines of the fields around us as he must have—miles and miles of nowhere to hide, more space than he'd seen in weeks. I pulled over and slowly turned the car around.

"How about pizza instead?"

"God, yes," he said, covering his face with his hands in agitation and leaving them there for a long time. I watched him carefully over the new few weeks, and he knew I was watching him. I fought the urge to reach out and touch him all the time, for whose reassurance I don't know.

More things leaked out over time. One afternoon we were hiking in Sequoia National Park and Ross started pointing out plants you could eat and places you could hide. If you've got your field spade or a knife, evidently, you can scratch out a shallow trough and bury yourself in leaves and dirt. In snow, there are ways of covering your tracks and carving out a shelter. In sand, there are ways of using a parachute to build camouflage. "You can hide pretty easily in lots of exposed-seeming places," he said, "as long as you don't move or look like a human body."

If SERE was to teach Ross how to hide, how to separate within himself to protect what was most valuable, even under extreme duress, then life as a military spouse was teaching me a faint echo of the relationship equivalent—how do you protect the core of intimacy at the heart of a marriage while at the same time welcoming into it all the possibilities of a life at war?

Was this what I signed up for?

CHAPTER 5

Both of my grandfathers served in World War II, and they provided me with two contrary versions of what military service was like. Both were young and poor, and both volunteered—among boys their age, it was what everyone was doing, going off to fight the "good war." My maternal grandfather, Ray, was an Army Air Corps pilot who, due to a delay in training caused by an injury to his hand, missed the opportunity to see combat and instead served out his time stateside as an instructor pilot. Ray was full of wartime stories of high adventure, dangerous pranks, and bucking against authority, most too good to be entirely true. My paternal grandfather, Bill, was an Army infantryman who fought in the Pacific theater in New Guinea and Luzon and was later stationed in Japan after the atom bombs dropped. He never talked about the war. Growing up, I knew he still had nightmares, and I'd once seen the long whitish scar running along his side when he was changing shirts in a hotel room, but I was twenty-one years old before I worked up the courage to ask him anything about it.

He told me the scar was from a mortar blast that killed the man huddled right beside him in the same foxhole, his best friend at the time. The skirmish was over a stolen American howitzer that Japanese troops were using to fire at Bill's platoon. After the blast that killed his friend, Bill's gun jammed, but he managed to fix it and pick off the men firing the howitzer. His platoon had been decimated, but since they had recaptured the howitzer, Bill's commanding officer told him he was putting him in for a Silver Star. While Bill was at a field hospital getting his wound treated, the rest of his platoon, along with the commanding officer, were killed, and any talk of awards for valor died with them. I asked if he felt disappointed. "I wasn't over there looking for medals," was all he would say. He spent another year doing long-range reconnaissance patrols, the kind of ten- and twenty-mile hikes behind enemy lines that get assigned with a loose expectation of return, before boarding a boat headed to Japan, part of a fleet of men slated to be the first wave of a ground assault on the Japanese mainland. It was considered a death sentence, but then came the blasts at Hiroshima and Nagasaki. Bill got assigned to walk patrols in Hiroshima after it was leveled. "It looked like a cornfield plowed under. A whole city." He was twenty-one years old, my age at the time of our conversation.

Ray and Bill both raised their families a half mile from each other in Snyder, Texas. They knew of each other, as families in small towns do, and some of their children attended school together. Bill started out as a telephone lineman, which was how he met my grandmother Rosa, who was working as a switchboard operator and helping to support her chaotic and embattled family of eleven. Bill and Rosa had three kids—my father, Royce, was the middle son who never felt like he fit in anywhere. My dad played baseball in high school, drank, and got into trouble until the drama coach, Jerry Worsham, took him under his wing and convinced him to try acting. My dad had finally found his niche, a place big enough to allow him to embrace his contradictory nature, the unabashed lover of poetry and literature mixed in with what I've always considered the slightly thuggish streak that later allowed him to blend in with oilfield roughnecks.

After his plan to get an engineering degree on the GI Bill failed, Ray joined his father in starting up a brick plant. He'd met my grandmother Mary during the war while he was stationed near Syracuse, New York, and transplanted her, after a long campaign of fictions and embellishments, to west Texas. My mother, Kathy, was number three of six children born to them, two years behind my father in school, and often felt lost in the shuffle, overshadowed by the drama of Mary and Ray's tumultuous union in a house full of children and yelling. She grew to be six feet tall, a shy outcast and striking beauty with dark, expressive eyes who blossomed, like my father before her, under Jerry Worsham's tutelage. Cast as romantic leads in a play the summer after my mom finished high school, my parents fell in love learning the lines of Lord Bothwell and Mary, Queen of Scots.

The path that led to their marriage four years later in Aberdeen, Scotland, was anything but straightforward. My dad was looking for a way out—out of Snyder, out of Texas, out of everything that seemed to lie ahead of him, including Vietnam, where his low draft number threatened to send him immediately upon graduation. In those four years, he managed to pack in a breakup with my mom; a preemptive enlistment in the Navy for Officer Candidate School to avoid being drafted into the Army; a failed engagement to another woman; a failed physical, for bee sting allergies, which then excluded him from all military service and nullified his OCS application; a brief stint in law school, from which he dropped out and moved back home with his parents; and jobs as both a plumber's apprentice and a ditch digger. In the summer of 1972, he needed a win, badly, and he got two. First, he and my mom got back together, and second, a successful interview with an oil company looking for liberal arts graduates (teachable, they reasoned, and likely looking for work) meant he was soon leaving the country for oil rig work offshore in the North Sea near Scotland. "Halfheartedly," as my mother remembers ("humbly," if you hear it from my dad), he asked her to come with him.

By the time I found myself sketching out the first tentative lines of what life would be like married to a man in the Navy, I had all of these stories in the back of my head, along with a lifetime of being raised in the liberal stronghold of Austin, Texas, and a brief and deeply unsettling interlude of living in Saudi Arabia as an oil company dependent. Military service, in my family history, had started out as something my grandfathers took on because they were physically able and of age, and they did it during a war the country considered a shared effort for a noble cause, one for which everyone sacrificed something, even if it was just rubber or silk or sugar. For their children, my parents, being a soldier was a fate dealt out by lottery, and war, its causes and its course, was a topic of passionate debate and even riot. My understanding of the underlying principles of military service, and of the costs it exacted, was contradictory, full of silence, nightmares, embellishments, and changes of course.

Ross came from a similar history but somehow felt clearer about the issues on the table when he signed up for service. He pledged an oath to an ostensibly all-volunteer force, and our war turned into wars that kept spreading past the next promised "drawing down." This modern military, the more I got to know it, felt like a separate, and largely invisible, society all its own. My life as a Navy spouse rested on paradigms that shifted even as I was building them. "You knew what you signed up for" was a phrase I heard often and it infuriated me. It was a callous denial of empathy, a distancing move that drew a clear line between the people who made up the majority of the country and the people who did its fighting.

More than that, it was a jab in a tender place, the place where I *had* signed up for something when I made a promise to support Ross as his wife, but how could I—how could anyone—know exactly what challenges were going to be thrown our way? Sometimes it seemed like two different tasks whose interests were not necessarily aligned, supporting him in the microcosm of our marriage and supporting him in the larger world where he was a military pilot. Ross and I didn't always agree—in either of these worlds—and where he saw things in a more black-and-white way, I remained confused, certain only that the harder I looked, the more gray I saw.

CHAPTER 6

For the first year we lived in Lemoore, and Ross was learning to fly the Super Hornet, I was a free agent when it came to wives' club membership and responsibilities, though not by choice. After waiting weeks for an official welcome e-mail, I gently broached the topic of a wives' group with a woman I met at a party, who told me point-blank that I should run the other direction, that the group was toxic and that no new members were being contacted in an effort to quarantine the dysfunction. I asked Ross if I shouldn't perhaps contact someone else, someone more impartial, and he cocked an eyebrow at me and asked, "If someone told you a whole room full of people had the stomach flu, why would you keep trying to get in?"

"Fine," I said, "I know how to be the new kid. I'll just find my own friends."

Step one: get a job. Tomato inspector, prison librarian, community sexual health educator, and college English department secretary. These were the four jobs on my short list of careers in central California, culled from the local newspaper and a methodical search of the HR sites of companies within my area, a broad swath of rural farmland just south of Fresno. As Ross turned his attention to his training, I polished four wildly different cover letters and resumes. I was familiar with the drill by now—focus on skill sets learned and play up the words "adaptable" and "versatile," glossing over the short tenures and telltale locations that might out me as a military wife likely to relocate on short notice. By now I had decided that my writing career might always be something totally separate from my job. I could earn money anywhere doing anything and then live and write in the margins.

After two bleak months in which I heard nothing back from anyone and came up with an even weirder list of B-string careers, Planned Parenthood offered me an interview. A three-person panel explained to me that the job required a certain "social ease," a general comfort with people that allowed one to stroll up to strangers at bus stops and community events and start conversations about sexually transmitted infections and the ease and convenience of getting tested. The tall Latino man at the end of the table suggested I role-play a conversation with him where I would approach him at a city park and open a dialogue about chlamydia, incorporating some of the bullet points from the fact sheet he slid across the table. The only ones that jumped out at me were: (1) the Central Valley had the highest rate of the infection in California and (2) the test no longer required that a tiny bristled brush be inserted into the head of the penis. I spread my fingers on the table, noticing that the lube from my condom demonstration question was still making my hands sticky, and finally confessed that I had no idea how to start the conversation, but if they could teach me a skill like that, I would consider it a huge character strength. I didn't get the job.

Similarly unimpressed with me were the prison system and the tomato factory, which, honestly, was a relief since both would have relied heavily on my atrophied Spanish language skills. When a well-known Southern novelist from the college English department called me one morning two months later, I was deep into an unemployment funk and filling out an application to the local hardware store, knowing I was facing stiff competition from the local teenagers. "I'm sorry it's taken us a while to get moving on this," he drawled apologetically. "I was just hoping you hadn't gone off and gotten a job at McDonald's already." We both laughed as though the idea were preposterous and arranged for an interview. In the meantime, I was to send him some writing samples. My plan was to worm my way into the university as an employee, get in-state residency, and then use my employee education benefit to take one graduate class at a time, chipping away at a master's in rhetoric and composition until I finally had the credentials and experience to teach full freshman seminars, not just writing labs, at community colleges. The novelist, my new boss, waved his hand dismissively at all of this. "You need to be in the MFA program," he said. "And not in a year. Now."

And thus did my own training regimen finally start. For three years I had followed Ross across the country as he crammed his head full of weather patterns, the physics of flight, and emergency procedures, three years of wild flight student parties where guys set off M-80s in their rental house bathrooms and smashed watermelons all over the kitchen because they didn't care if they got the deposit back. I was finally claiming "study nights" of my own,

burying myself in mountains of essays and memoirs, and dragging Ross to poetry readings and book signings where the crowd
still drank just as hard but also had conversations about the National Book Award. It was exhilarating, finally being the one to
introduce Ross to new people and explain shop talk to him instead of the other way around. It also felt like the balance of power
in our relationship was shifting into something closer to equilib-
rium. He had his goal that he was working for and I had mine—
not just a placeholder job, not just a means of treading water while
I waited for the next relocation—but finally a reason for me to be
where I was. It wasn't just that Ross's calendar was no longer the
only one we lived by, and it wasn't just that my job neatly covered
my tuition with a little left over so that I wasn't draining the
household income to follow my own path. It was the difference
between making the best of an accident and deciding there was
actually a purpose for my being in California. I found power in
that purpose, and it made the weeks Ross wasn't around easier
to bear.

It also meant I was finally making some friends, even if they
lived an hour's drive from the town I was currently calling home.
I had an entirely separate community in which I could stake out
an identity, one in which it didn't matter a bit what Ross did,
where his call sign was not some kind of required recitation to
help people place who I was. In Lemoore, though, I was back at
square one, the memory of the awkward party of instructors'
wives in Corpus Christi fresh in my mind. I found myself wondering if I was ever going to fit in among Navy wives.

Jessie, my first best friend in the military community, was
hard to find. "Bendy Jessie" was a former ballerina turned podi-
atrist's assistant, with ice blue eyes, dark hair, and a freckled,

upturned nose and the hilarious and amazing habit of pulling physical stunts like one-armed push-ups and standing splits against the wall when she'd had a few drinks. She was five years younger than me, direct and practical, and wise in a way I sometimes found unnerving. Her boyfriend, Brad, was a gigantic, crew-cut Marine who had gone through advanced training with Ross in Kingsville, throughout which time Jessie had remained back home in Florida where she and Brad had met. They moved in together when Brad moved out to Lemoore, but it was another couple of months before we actually started hanging out.

Brad was keen to get Jessie and me together, and initially I resisted, seeing it as some kind of weird boyfriend-initiated playdate. The feeling, it turned out, was mutual, Jessie being naturally suspicious of Navy wives and still trying to find her bearings in a new town. Our friendship unfolded over dinners and drinks, first at both of our houses and then mostly at hers, and it quickly left the stiff, collegial bond shared by Ross and Brad in the dust. It was liberating, frankly, hanging out with someone whose significant other, as a Marine, wasn't in competition with Ross for grades or positions, the kind of competition it takes a lot of energy to ignore. Soon it was mostly me going over to hang out with Jessie and Brad, and then just me and Jessie going to the gym, or dress shopping in Fresno for the Hornet Ball, or getting riotously drunk on Tuaca at her house and playing dress-up with her old dance costumes. We could roll our eyes at the awkward encounters we each weathered on base, me as a wife unattached to a club and Jessie toeing the peculiarly sensitive line girlfriends walk, where other spouses tried politely to figure out who you were or where you belonged.

So it was bittersweet, I knew, when Brad proposed to her and our long talks started turning toward her wedding. I was happy for her, of course, but the wedding was part of the long-term future, a future that inevitably included Jessie and Brad's moving to another city and following the separate fork of a Marine aviation career, which would rarely, if ever, intersect with a Navy one again. We got a wedding invitation after they moved away, and I hung on to it even though some training exercise or our perpetually strained finances meant we'd RSVP'd regrets. It ached, watching on Facebook in the intervening years as Jessie and Brad raised a beautiful baby girl, and knowing that no matter how many times I hit "like" on her pictures, or exchanged short Messenger updates with her on our lives, our kids, and moves, we'd probably never again be as close as we were then, back when we both felt like outsiders in the community of military spouses.

The reality of close friendships among military wives is that they have a half-life, often one both members of the friendship calculate at the beginning—*how long are you here for and where are you likely headed next?* There is always that chance that fate and BUPERS (the Bureau of Naval Personnel and the mysterious hub from which relocation orders emanate) can reunite old friends, and indeed it's what we all hope for. "See you again soon," is the phrase this community uses instead of "good-bye." Still, every one of these friendships, no matter how dear they are, no matter how essential they feel to making it through a particular posting, can also feel like pouring your heart into building an elaborate sand castle. You know, at the end of the day, that the odds are excellent that you will lose this beautiful thing. It's not a reason not to build one—in fact, when they are at their best, friendships among military wives are so intimate and intense precisely because the tide is so reliable. We build fast and we take risks in how much we reveal and how deeply we trust, risks a normal friendship would take years to earn. While it's still standing, what we have built is wonderfully strong.

CHAPTER 7

The YouTube window expanded to full-screen mode and we stared at blackness. No sound came through the attached speakers except for occasional radio transmissions, the low whine of electrical instruments and wind, and the jagged, irregular sound of someone trying not to hyperventilate. Taken from a tiny camera mounted in the cockpit of an F/A-18 landing on a carrier at night, this video was a pretty accurate vision of what Ross would see for the first time in less than three weeks. We hunched in front of the computer, the overhead light off for effect.

"Two one zero. Left of course, correcting. Four miles." Still nothing but blackness.

"That's the approach controller," Ross said quietly. "He's in the air traffic control center on the boat watching and talking to this guy on the radio." Ross was using the common aviation parlance for an aircraft carrier—dismissive, belittling, this massive moving city in the water is called a "boat" by the aviation community and a "ship" by everyone else. Partly this has to do with perspective—

from a mile away, it *is* small—but it was also about a different kind of perspective as well. Already, he was learning the disdain of the aviation community for its surface warfare counterparts.

The pilot's acknowledgment came over the speakers. "Two one zero."

"I don't see anything," I said. A small, wry smile crossed Ross's lips. Carrier qualifications were the last hurdle he had to clear before moving from the RAG to his first fleet squadron, and in many ways, it felt like the final high-stakes culmination of the previous three years of flight school.

Seconds later, the approach controller again:

"Two one zero, slightly below glide path, slightly right of course. Two miles."

"Two one zero."

And then a slight flicker, like a dying firefly. Barely four pixels across, I confused it at first with lint on the computer screen, so I reached out and wiped at it. It wobbled uncertainly and refused to resolve into a shape.

"Those are the tower lights," Ross said.

"Two miles? That's all he can s—" And before I could finish, a warning tone blared. "What's that?" The tone sounded like a tiny British ambulance, like the kind of sound Nintendo games make when Mario accidentally leaps into a flaming pit.

"His RADALT. It's an altimeter warning when you descend below a certain altitude."

More transmissions: "Three one zero, ACLS lock-on, say needles."

"Now they're talking to the guy behind him."

This seemed unfair to me. Why should 210 have to hear about everyone stacking up behind him? What if he got confused about which message was for him? The breathing sped up, shuddered between breaths.

"Two one zero, slightly below glide path, on course, three-quarter mile. Call the ball."

"Two one zero rhinoballsixfive." 210 was smashing his words together and breathing hard, but his voice was pitched low and even. He sounded like someone quietly trying to alert you that there's a rattlesnake in his lap.

"Roger ball. You're a little low."

"That's the Landing Signals Officer taking over," said Ross. "He's standing on the back of the boat watching this guy come in." The LSO sounded like he was sitting in front of a nice fireplace with a snifter of brandy in his hand. His voice was rich and deep and calm. "A little low" sounded like a minor condition, something completely expected and within the normal course of nature and the world, and not a warning that 210 might want to correct his course in order not to smash into the back of the carrier in a giant fireball.

The tower lights were still faint and tiny, enough to confirm that something was out there in all that blackness, but thoroughly unconvincing in conjuring images of safety and massiveness, of a landing area, of a bunk and a hot meal somewhere beneath the deck, a small city plowing through the dark.

The breathing was fast and jagged and all of a sudden, *there it was!* Like a highway lit up at night with small dashed lines reflecting the center line. The whole thing wavered uncertainly, racing toward 210, and us, and Ross pointed to the far left of the screen and said, "There's the ball," just as it disappeared. I couldn't tell how far above the highway we were and everything was speeding up and getting louder.

"Little come left." It was Lord Calm Voice in his parlor again, and 210, now sounding like he was in the middle of an asthma attack, dutifully dipped the wing of the jet slightly left milliseconds before all the lights leapt and scattered over the screen, the engines roared in protest, and a long, rasping gasp was punched out of 210's chest as his tailhook caught the wire. From where I sat, it looked like the camera had been punted. Radio chatter continued, but I couldn't hear any of it. I found myself leaning forward, my nails digging into the fabric of my running pants.

The screen went black again and I could hear someone called 103 being told to set himself up for the approach. More tiny dim lights appeared and rotated slowly along the bottom of the screen. 210 was regaining control of his breathing, though it was still shuddery sounding, and he'd apparently gotten the wherewithal to start thinking about moving off the runway and parking his jet. This seemed like asking someone to steer a flaming eighteen-wheeler at top speed through a garden gate, stop within ten feet, and then neatly parallel park because other flaming eighteen-wheelers were right behind.

Ross was laughing—apparently this was exciting or motivating or something—and all I could say was, "*Fuck* that."

The group of students headed out to the boat for carrier quals traditionally grew out mustaches together, so when I kissed Ross good-bye and wished him luck, it was a weird State Trooper version of my husband I was sending off, one who looked both comical and grim. It wasn't the carrier qualification I was worried about, but what came after. Assignment to a fleet squadron meant one of three locations—Lemoore, Virginia Beach, or Atsugi, Japan, an hour's train ride from Tokyo. I had a one-in-three chance of staying in my job and the MFA program, and the prospect of losing what little foothold I'd gained sickened me. So it was a complete surprise when Ross called me two days later, stricken, to say, "I DQ'd." Disqualified. The word didn't make sense when applied to him, and I must have made it worse when I asked him to repeat it.

"Are you okay? What happened?" Qualifying takes twenty good passes, twelve in daylight, eight at night, with about three days total to complete them. Ross had only three night passes to go when he started to "bolter," or miss the wire. His fuel ran lower with each unsuccessful pass and finally he'd been directed to divert and land ashore to refuel.

He wasn't the only one to run into trouble during that trip. Another student, a friend of ours, evidently had a close call so scary that even asking more than one person about it years later, I ran into a wall of silence. Not moving beyond this qualifying stage isn't uncommon. I've heard anecdotes of at least two pilots who sailed smoothly through every part of flight school only to balk when it was time to land on the boat, or do it once and then calmly shut down the engines and refuse to go back out again.

"Launches" and "traps" create the kinds of forces on the human body rarely found outside of vehicle collisions. During a launch, a massive steam-powered catapult hidden belowdecks slingshots the jet off the front of the boat with such speed—zero to roughly 180 miles per hour in two seconds—that the otolith organ, the little bowl of jelly in the brain pan that orients the body in space, plasters itself against the back of its chamber and screams to the brain that the body is on its back, shooting straight up. The disorientation can be so strong that the natural impulse is to push the jet's stick forward and bring its nose down—directly into the water. To address this risk, a pilot leaves his left hand on the throttle, pushed to max, and salutes the shooter on deck with his right before reaching up to grab a stationary handle called the "towel bar," leaving the stick completely untended. For the first few seconds after it begins its climb, the jet flies itself. The launch, evidently, yields one of the most potent adrenaline hits there is, strong enough in most cases to balance out the trap, and in particular, the near-blind act of faith that is the night trap.

A trap involves threading the needle of speed, glide path, angle, altitude, and lineup all while listening to an LSO on the radio, reading the instruments, and looking for the tiny light on the boat called the "meatball" or the "ball," accurate only when you're perfectly lined up. A hook lowered from the back of the jet searches the boat's deck for one of four retractable wires laid across it, ideally grabbing the third from the back, the "three wire." The jet makes its pass at full speed in case the hook misses the wire, so the jolt when it does catch is brutal—something like 150 miles per hour to zero in two seconds. Certain kinds of corrective eye surgery used to be forbidden because it was worried that the force of the trap would cause the altered, unanchored cornea to separate.

Many more lives are at risk in the complex choreography of bodies running back and forth in color-coded jerseys on deck. An aircraft carrier deck is commonly called "the most dangerous three and a half acres in the world." Fuelers in purple gas up the jets; plane captains in brown inspect the exteriors; ordnance personnel, or "ordies," in red handle the missiles and bombs, loading and unloading them from hard points on the undersides of the wings; "greenshirts" maintain the catapult and the arresting wires; plane directors in yellow guide taxiing jets to the catapult and use hand signals or lighted wands to run through checklists with the pilot; a catapult officer, or "shooter," also in yellow, operates the catapult; and "blueshirts" tow the jets, chock the wheels, and chain the jets back to the deck. Safety observers and medical personnel wear white, as do the LSOs, who have a safety net suspended just below the deck and off to one side so they can jump out of the way if it looks like a jet is about to hit the boat. In the base of the tower, the "handler" coordinates all movement on the deck with the aid of the "Ouija board," a flight deck in miniature with little planes and colored tokens to account for all the action outside. Watching over everything and calling the shots on the deck and in the landing pattern is the "air boss."

It's an environment that doesn't tolerate failure. Ross took it hard. He had one more chance to pass, and to prepare for it he would complete another round of FCLPs, field carrier landing practices, at the runway in Lemoore. In the meantime, I was discovering his biggest weakness, a debilitating frustration from making a mistake. He dragged around the house during the day, distracted and silent, and then at night he tossed and turned in the bed, kicking off the covers and heaving big sighs. All of my reassurances felt hollow in the face of this death-defying stunt he would have to repeat, and when I tried to bury myself in work and school, it was with the knowledge that if he succeeded, there was a very good chance I might have to quit both to move again.

I'm not sure why I got the invitation one day to come out and watch a round of practice landings with the landing signals officer at the runway. I know other wives who have done it, and the only thing I can guess is that it's something like Lady Redhawk Day, a rare chance to see some real details about an event that was having a huge impact on our lives at home. It was generous and compassionate, this opportunity to hang out with the LSO helping Ross to get out of his own head.

I met Ross out in the hangar parking lot as he was "about to walk," which is different from walking because the end destination is the plane you'll fly that day. Otherwise the movement is the same. He tossed me a package of earplugs and gave me directions to get to the ready room where I was to ask for a man named Frumba. I carried a notepad and pencil, prepared to pepper him with questions.

Inside, I approached the duty desk and said, "Hi, I'm looking for Frumba Hines," and then immediately blushed when I figured out the call sign. Call signs are professional nicknames, official shorthand identities that have an uncanny way of insinuating themselves into off-duty life. They are assigned by colleagues, and the Navy's approach to assigning them differs significantly from that of the Air Force. In the Air Force, you get to be "Slasher" or "Diablo." In the Navy, you get caught one time in Rollerblades and you're "Fruit Boots" for the rest of your career.

"Hi," a tall sandy-haired, square-jawed man said, walking over from across the room and extending his hand, "I'm Cade. We're going to be headed to the left runway today. There's a nasty crosswind, but that's the runway with the most up-to-date set of landing lights."

A white van ferried us out to the LSO shack, which looked like a little greenhouse, maybe where retired people would grow orchids if it weren't out in the middle of a barren field and six feet away from a runway. There was a sliding glass door on the east and west ends, and the whole thing was no larger than a typical guest bathroom. The plywood floor was stained from water leaks and tobacco spit, and there was just enough room for three tall stools. A shelf mounted on the back wall held two radios, labeled "top radio" and "bottom radio," a box of Post-its, and several faded tubes of sunscreen. Two tan telephone sets sat just beneath the shelf on top of a large metal cabinet that looked like a mini-fridge but had something to do with turning on the radios to the tower. Cade/Frumba flipped some switches and picked up a handset.

"Tower, Paddles. Radio check."

"What does 'Paddles' mean?" I asked, and he explained that in the old days of carrier aviation, the planes were tail draggers built with the engines up front. In order to land, the nose of the plane had to be cocked up so that the tailhook could catch the wires. This position made it impossible to see the deck out the front of the plane over the massive engines. So a guy stood on the edge of the back of the boat with things that looked like Ping-Pong paddles and did a little dance so the pilot could crane his neck to look out his side window and see what he had to do to land. Each paddle represented a wing, and the first LSOs were like birds of paradise, dancing out their meaning as a physical representation of the plane itself. Left paddle low meant dip your left wing; both paddles flapping up meant add power and get higher; kicking either foot meant add rudder left or right. Frumba demonstrated the dance. It looked ridiculous for how serious and dangerous it must have been. But the name stuck, and now the LSO reports himself to the tower as Paddles.

"See these painted lines?" He motioned to a huge white box, roughly six hundred feet long and painted at a slight angle against the vertical stretch of runway. "That represents the carrier."

It looked small to me. I tried to imagine it surrounded by miles and miles of ocean, how it must look like a postage stamp from the air during the day. I couldn't imagine it at night.

"You don't land on the boat straight on. The boat's landing area is at an angle to account for the tower, so you can't just line up with the boat and be done with it. You've got to fly at it at an angle. The tough part is that the place you're aiming for is always moving away from you, but it's also pitching, rolling, and heaving, and that's one thing we can't simulate out here. When they land on the boat, they'll hear all kinds of calls to correct for that movement, so I go ahead and do those calls out here just because I want them to respond immediately to my voice." He grinned. "It's kind of like training a dog."

From the top of a shelf, Frumba pulled out a stick about the length of a billy club, the handle of which was wrapped in electrical tape, with a thumb button on top and trigger button just below on the front of the stick.

"This is called the 'pickle switch.' It controls the light display. See?" Frumba showed me the different options, which, along with his voice on the radio, were meant to communicate to pilots what the dancing man of yore did with his Ping-Pong paddles. The thumb button activated the "cut lights," two sets of green lights, which meant "add power; climb." The trigger button lit up the red "wave-off lights," which meant either, "you're doing bad, go away," or in the case of a blocked landing area, "wave-off, foul deck."

Frumba waved the end of the stick over toward the road across the runway and out to the east, where, about a hundred yards away, about six cars were lined up in a tiny parking lot, open to the public and to families, and at any other time the closest I could get to watching practice landings. "These are the fans all watching your man." My man. I bridled a little at the cheeseball wife-line, but I also felt a hot surge of pride. Other people *got* what Ross did and were interested enough to pull over and watch. I was instantly embarrassed at the rush and tangle of my thoughts and refocused on what Frumba was saying about where the planes would touch down before taking off again.

He pointed to a rubber-blackened area about eight feet square on the runway just outside the sliding door. "We're imagining the wires, so I want to see his wheels hit right about there. Too far that way"—he pointed south down to the start of the runway—"and he's low. He could risk hitting the back of the boat or catching a one or two wire. Too much that way"—he pointed north back over our shoulders—"and he's too high. He might catch a four wire or miss the wires entirely and go flying again." On the boat, every trap is graded and every grade is posted in the ready room—everyone knows who has the highest average and who's struggling.

The planes were lining up in a racetrack formation out in the sky. The sun was patchy and I could see clouds breaking to the south and shadows licking over the hills off to the west. Rain hit the closed glass door of the shack and the rumbling noise outside got deeper.

"Earplugs in?" Frumba asked, as the first plane passed the western door, getting ready to turn again and approach the runway on our east side. The radio came alive.

"Two zero five abeam, gear, flaps full, RADALT to the HUD."

Ross was first up. He sounded like a little old man on the radio, or a robot with low batteries, and he talked fast and serious and low pitched, not at all like his voice in person. Frumba responded in a quiet, melodic FM voice that shocked me.

"Welcome abeam, two zero five. Wind is east at fourteen knots. Charlie." Off the radio he told me, "Now, if I'm a betting man, I say we're going to see him pushed way out east now . . . but that's a pretty aggressive turn he's making. Good. He knows what I'm telling him." The plane approached and I was struck by how inelegant it looked grappling with the wind, its control surfaces fluttering like big metal feathers. It came in slightly flaring its nose high at us, trying to catch the push of the wind to find the perfect angle and speed, and then just outside the doors the tires smashed against the concrete and the engines roared as the plane took off again, its wheels only a hard smudge on the ground before lifting off again. The engine roar rattled in my chest and shook the glass in the shack's windows. I felt washed over with noise and momentum, exhilarated, and a little terrified, and I noticed I was gripping my pencil hard enough to risk snapping it. Frumba recorded a series of letters and parentheses in slots under which he'd written each pilot's last name. I wondered what they meant. Good or bad?

The next plane came around, and I could distinguish the radio call a little better. The pass was low and neat and in the engine roar this time I noticed Frumba was talking again in that quiet soothing voice, critiquing the pass while he recorded the codes. I watched about fifty passes. After ten, I started to see what Frumba meant when he'd mutter, off the radio, "Don't settle," meaning don't let the plane sink, or "Work it down, work it down." The more I watched, the more the landings seemed to vary, some coming in high and then drifting low at the last minute, some coming in too low and farting out little clouds of exhaust as the pilot tried to compensate by adding power. I pushed at the planes with my mind—*come down, come up, stay steady*—which was about the closest thing I'd done to praying in a long time.

"He's got the monkey skills down," Frumba remarked. "He just needs to relax, get his confidence back." I'd heard Ross use this term before. It referred to the physical movements of hands on stick and throttle.

On Ross's last pass, Frumba coached me to respond to his radio call for the ball by saying "Roger ball" in a kind of singsong cadence. When he pointed to me, I was to say at the last minute, "Wave off, wave off, foul deck," at which point Frumba would "pickle" the red lights and Ross would shove up on the throttles to keep from touching down and roar off again. Things went pretty much exactly as planned, except that I got a huge adrenaline rush from watching the approaching plane and practicing my line in my head and I ended up practically screaming it. In the moment, it was weirdly exhilarating that something I said caused a reaction that big. I couldn't help laughing in the shack and had to remind myself to shut my mouth when my big gaping smile started to ache. Later, another pilot in the pattern, a friend of ours, told me I scared the entire formation, who were used to concentrating on soothing voices that betrayed no emotion or urgency, except if you were seconds away from becoming a ball of fire.

When I thought about it later, there seemed a few obvious questions I could have asked Frumba in the spirit of rigorous inquiry, such as "Have you ever seen an accident?" or "Have you ever had to jump into the little emergency net on the boat?" The questions never even occurred to me. Being in fake reporter mode with my notebook and pencil was my best attempt at distancing myself from the stakes of what Ross was training for. There were still some things I didn't want to know.

I started having dreams about planes more and more during this time. There was one recurring one: In it, I was allowed somehow to go visit Ross on the aircraft carrier. When I got there I found that every square inch was devoted to massive mechanical tasks involving things that could crush and kill me, and there was no room for me in the living quarters. I had to huddle near the towering edge of the boat, where the drop to the water was six stories, below me all churning wake and blackness.

Later in the dream the Navy allowed me to fly with Ross, only I didn't get to be in the cockpit—I had to hang on to the nose and was secured there only by my grip on various inch-deep grooves. I faced Ross in the cockpit, like a bug crawling on his windshield, and between the space of his helmet and oxygen mask I could see only his eyes. He did a preflight check, scanning all the instruments with his focused gaze, which continually jumped back to meet mine. I could read concern there, clearly, but then the engines spooled up and men hooked the catapult shuttle to the plane and I started to understand that this would be way too fast—*Why is anyone letting me do this? There's no way I'll be able to hang on.*

And then suddenly there was a noise so loud I felt it in my chest, wind like a wall and pressure and pain all at once, and we were out over the water, shoving higher and higher, my grip changing, him pulling the stick back and climbing but then banking hard to one side, unbelievably hard, in one of those physics-bending moves that the Super Hornet does where it looks improbable and wrong even to people watching on the ground, and our eyes met again and I pleaded *pleasepleasepleaseI'msoscared* but my words were ripped out of my mouth before they could form and he knew, he got it, every bit of him got it and felt for me, but there it was: he couldn't stop. He couldn't make it stop until it was time to land, and even *that* might kill me if I made it until then. *Hang on*, his eyes said, *please hang on*.

Ross redeemed himself with an above-average second round of carrier quals. Added to the list of reasons to celebrate was the fact that he'd been picked up by a fleet squadron in Lemoore for his first sea tour, a three-year period in which I could keep working and finish out my MFA. The squadron he joined was just entering its cycle of three month-long "work-ups"—a month home, a month gone, another month home, another gone, and so on—in preparation for a six-month deployment. I was so grateful for the chance to remain in one place long enough to get something accomplished that I didn't think too much about the future deployment. Instead, I turned my attention to meeting the other women in the squadron's wives' club, hoping to find a friend.

Stella, a knockout beauty with a glorious waterfall of long blond hair, was probably the last person I expected to stroll over and pluck one of the Mexican beers I'd brought to my first wives' club meeting. Everyone else had brought tastefully arranged appetizers and cookies and arrayed them on the dining room table. I'd brought a six-pack.

"Where do you think we can find a bottle opener in this joint?"

I had been hanging back at the kitchen counter, smiling awkwardly near several conversations and trying to arrange the handful of limes I'd brought to go with the beer, wondering if I was really supposed to be here or if this was going to be another disaster like in Corpus Christi. Within the first few minutes of chatting with Stella she dropped an F-bomb into a story about driving her preschool-age daughter around to various activities, and when she covered her mouth in mock horror and apology, I knew I'd found her, my next good friend.

In another stroke of incredible luck, it turned out Ross and Jake, Stella's husband, had already become good friends and were eager to get us all together for dinner. Up until now, Ross and I had weathered a series of mismatched friendships with couples, one of us always lagging behind in our connection and enthusiasm, but Stella and Jake were a different story. As our friendship with them developed over time, I found a sense of belonging I'd thought was impossible for me in a military community. Over the next three years, Stella and I would go through a deployment together, travel to Singapore and back, and watch her two kids grow from toddlers to schoolchildren. By including me in the rhythm of her daily life when the guys were gone, Stella showed me how the next act could go, the one still somewhere off in the future where Ross and I may or may not agree that it was finally time to have a baby.

For now, there was still a lot to learn, including how to say good-bye to our husbands for half of the coming year. Ross asked if I wanted to drive down to San Diego after his last work-up to see the USS *John C. Stennis*, the aircraft carrier that would be home to his squadron on its deployment of the western Pacific. I was on the fence about going until Stella suggested I come with her and the kids. "It'll be noisy," she said by way of apology, but it was noise I was looking for. I needed a distraction if I was going to do this, something to keep me in the present and not stuck with the memories of another port city, twenty years in the past.

CHAPTER 8

I was ten years old the first time I saw an oil rig up close. The P-82 had been towed into port for repairs in Galveston, Texas, and the four of us—Mom, Dad, Doug, and me—went down to the docks to check it out. I remember this being sort of a last-minute detour on our way home from a rare family vacation, an educational experience my mom jollied my dad into and about which he seemed less than enthusiastic. Years later, knowing a little of the backstory on this particular rig, I can imagine it now through my father's eyes, this hulking, decrepit structure whose deficiencies had been ignored while it was a working rig pulling in revenue, but in port for millions of dollars' worth of expensive repairs now that the company had been bought out by a foreign firm. It was a time when OPEC was playing with the price of a barrel of oil again, and many companies were vulnerable to foreign buyouts. The P-82 was also the site of a long-standing personality conflict between my dad and another man representing one of the rig's contractors, a man he later described as the only true sociopath he'd ever met. The man was a known problem, but, like all the other things broken on the P-82, something my dad was encouraged to make do with until a replacement could be found.

I knew none of this at the time, just as my dad knew nothing of the fact that less than a year after our tour of his old rig, his company would lay him off after seventeen years. My dad maintained a separation between work and home so profound that I struggled to explain what he did for a living, and never knew how to interpret the reactions of surprise I got from my friends and their parents when they asked. I got the impression that we were some kind of novelty, and that my dad working offshore fell somewhere on the spectrum between quaint and shameful, the operative question behind such a career choice being "Why?"

Since he commuted from Austin to wherever his rig was working at the time (during my childhood, most frequently in the Gulf of Mexico), we never met anyone else who worked on rigs, let alone their families. The closest I came to confirming the existence of my dad's coworkers was answering occasional phone calls to the house from guys with names like Bigfoot and 'Bama, who shouted into the receiver and with whom my dad held long, laughing conversations in which he used phrases like "*that stupid sonuvabitch.*" I wouldn't have been able to articulate the distinctions between blue-collar work and white-collar work then, or known what to make of the fact that my dad's collar was actually bright orange, but I knew enough to get angry and defensive when my friends balked at our strange, movable holiday plans or the possibility that my dad was missing my birthday for the third year in a row, and I learned to wrap my missing him into a tight ball and never mention it.

Around this time, I learned to forge my parents' signatures. It was less an act of delinquency than a parlor trick I thought might one day come in handy. My mother's signature required speed and a loose handling of the pen, a momentum and half focus probably necessary for keeping one eye on the kids in the checkout line and the other on the mounting total and its meaning for the bank account. My father's signature was more challenging, a squat, angular carving whose pressure drove a trough into the paper and whose slashing final *s* looped back and crossed a *t* six letters back. To do it, I had to bear down with my upper arm and grip the pen in my fist like I was trying to strangle it.

I remember this because it was my first real insight into my father's character at a time when I was desperate to find him, to understand why he left all the time and who he was when he was gone. I looked in his side of my parents' closet, in its dark, leather-reeking neatness. He took up about a third as much space as my mother, whose bright, soft, flowing fabrics poked out at all angles and smelled like lavender. I looked in the one drawer where he kept his spare rig coveralls, tightly rolled in neat bundles, the fire-retardant ones with "STARNES" stitched across the back of the shoulders in reflective tape so he could be seen at night, or in a gale, something for a searchlight to pick up if he went over the side. Everywhere I looked, I saw my mom, a loose, pervasive presence, covering our world from corner to corner. My dad, tightly compartmentalized, a coiled spring, the driving force ruling the calendar, was much harder to find.

The year of the P-82 was when I began to notice my father's depression, but as a kid, my ability to understand what I was seeing was limited. I was used to him taking long naps in the first few days of being home, but when I caught him staring at the wall above the television during his baseball games, and saw that runs and errors were accumulating on both sides without comment or reaction from him, I knew something was wrong. When he was "in a funk," as my mother called it, there were no games of catch in the front yard, no trivia questions at dinner, and he seemed irritable, much more likely to snap at me and my brother for making too much noise. It was hard to pin down exactly what was going on because it didn't look like what I pictured as "sad"—it was more like hearing an odd whine in a motor whose sound I usually didn't register. It spooked me. I remember coming up to him lying on his side on the couch one evening, thinking I would wake him for dinner, and finding that his eyes were open, and that when I spoke he didn't answer. He didn't even blink.

Visiting the P-82 was a complicated kind of vindication. It was physical proof that rigs existed, and it was something real to scowl at for having taken him away from us, but it was also impressive in its sheer mass, in the power of its silent machinery and the perilous heights of its creaking derrick. To hear my dad explain it, when the rig was fully operational, you had to know exactly what you were doing and where you were headed at any particular moment to avoid the very real possibility of being whacked in the back by a giant swinging piece of pipe or crushed in a massive set of tongs.

We had to reach out from the side of the dock and grab hold of a metal ladder attached to one of the pylons and climb to reach the first deck, and I remember being exhilarated at the possibility of falling into the scummy dock water. I asked my dad if I could chip off one of the pink and lavender barnacles crusted to the side of the column and he said if I could see myself chipping off barnacles all day with a long-handled scraper, I might make a decent roustabout. The rest of our short tour involved a lot of climbing, a lot of peering over massive drop-offs at giant machinery, and the sickening vertigo that comes from watching the water under the grating at our feet. We finished up by looking at Dad's quarters, a small, metal-walled, fluorescent-lit room with a twin bed and some dented metal cabinets. He surveyed the room with a kind of tired scowl and wouldn't come past the doorway.

"This is where you slept?" I asked, suddenly feeling really sorry for him. The drilling floor wasn't far away. There was no way this room would ever be quiet when the rig was operational.

"For the little time that I got for sleeping?" Dad said. "Yeah, this was it."

"But . . . what about all your stuff? Did you ever . . ." The words were drying up in my mouth as I realized how silly they sounded. "Did you ever decorate the place? Like, hang up pictures?"

"No," he said. "Every time I left, another guy was coming off the helicopter to take my place. You've got to understand—this wasn't a place I spent much time."

We left soon after, and I spent the long drive home wrestling with a knot of emotions I couldn't untangle. When I was little, I had pictured him being away at sea in something more like a pirate ship's quarters, somewhere with a round porthole window where he could spend time staring out at the water and missing all of us. I'd seen an animated movie that had informed much of my thinking about the distance between my dad and me when he was at work, and how we thought of each other. In it, a Russian immigrant mouse named Fievel sings to the night sky and his scattered family, "And even though I know how very far apart we are, it helps to think we might be wishing on the same bright star." From what I'd seen of the P-82, life at work was stressful, loud, and exhausting, and there wasn't much space for anything else. The realization that my father had far less time to miss me than I did for him hurt like a gut punch.

The day before Stella and I drove to San Diego I got all my hair cut off. At the time, I said it was on impulse, just one of those times when you need a change, but the truth was that I've never been that impulsive. Work-ups had been like a slow fade between Ross and me. I could feel him changing gears, making preparations to unplug from home life for an extended period. The haircut, from below my shoulders to a pixie, was my attempt to shed the identity of someone sad and about to get left behind and to morph into someone energetic and capable, someone who met adventure head-on and had no time for moping.

Stella and I met up with the guys at the Navy Lodge on North Island, where the sudden shock of my new haircut caused Ross to pause a couple of beats before he said he liked it. The two of us took a walk on the beach not saying much while Stella and Jake were occupied with rigging up a complicated structure of light-blocking blankets around their youngest son's Pack 'n Play. I envied their busyness and how having little kids seemed to create its own small world of regular emergencies, a world that left no room for prolonged thought. At dinner that night, I let the adult conversation float over my head as I drew crayon butterflies and dragons for the kids.

The next morning, Ross and I showed up at the *Stennis* just moments after an improvised "Hajji attack" meant to simulate a perimeter breach for the sailors who act as the boat's security in port. The air was still electric and every time someone called me "ma'am" it was with the overly loud, sharp edge of hyperalertness. Fake blood was spattered all over the ground and the enlisted boat crew leaving for liberty in their freshly unpacked civilian clothes tracked bloody footprints out of the port and into San Diego.

Aboard the ship, the first thing I noticed was the smell. Metal, grease, industrial solvents, fuel, rubber, exhaust—it smelled like my dad's coveralls when he unpacked his duffel bag from a hitch on the rig. It smelled, to me, exactly like loneliness and loss, and the perplexing sense that something happened to my dad each time he left, like there was a little less of him each time he came back. I knew that where the *Stennis* was headed was not an actual combat zone, but still I worried about where it would take Ross, or if he was the kind of guy who could lose himself in a place like this. We threaded our way belowdecks through an impossible number of identical hallways, up and down ladders, and past areas cordoned off for painting or repair, stepping up over the curved lip of the hatch each time we came to a doorway and angling our shoulders sideways each time we passed someone headed the opposite direction. Clatters and bangs echoed in between a variety of announcements from speakers mounted overhead.

Finally, Ross found his stateroom and ushered me in. "Stateroom" made it sound grand, but what we stood in looked a lot like an industrial janitor's closet. I knew I should have been grateful for the luxury of it compared to the vast room we'd seen full of human filing cabinets where enlisted sailors slept in bunks stacked four high. But I struggled to hide my horror when Ross flapped his arms and said triumphantly, "Look, I can stretch my arms all the way out!" We climbed up together into his bunk, which he'd outfitted with a foam-core mattress that he'd trimmed down from twin-sized so that it would fit. It was impossible to sit up without hitting my head on a network of interlaced white pipes. A narrow metal shelf with a fluorescent reading light stuck out from the wall next to the bed. I could see how it would afford just enough room for a few books and pictures. Ross turned on his side and wedged an arm in behind my head and started talking about plans he'd made for a full-length blackout curtain around the bunk's edge so his roommates could come and go, or play video games, without waking him. I stared at the shelf inches from my nose, remembering all the pictures and letters I'd sent my dad over the years in the hopes that he'd stick them up with a magnet somewhere and remember me. Suddenly I felt claustrophobic, practically clawing my way out over his reclined body.

"I need some air."

Up on the flight deck, Ross took me to see the catapult at the front of the boat that would launch him out over the waves. All I could see was a recessed track, kind of like the cable car tracks on the streets in San Francisco.

"This thing is loud. I could hear it all night long from my bunk, just a huge-ass piston slamming forward and then being reeled back in."

Then we went to see the arresting wires, all four laid out across the deck and covered in black grease.

"Remind me, which wire is the one you want to catch?"

"The three wire."

I knelt by the three wire, unabashedly reverent, and touched it lightly, asking it in my head to catch him and hold him, trying to infuse it with magnetism and a light he could see in the dark. I looked to the back of the boat, trying to picture the tiny landing lights of a plane a mile off in pitch blackness, and I told this wire to send out its message to the hook searching for it out over the waves. *Call him to you, hold him here.*

Ross led me around the rest of the boat—the wardroom dining areas, the "gerbil gyms," the ready room, where I checked out his little mail cubby and the bay of computers where he would be checking his e-mail, since there wasn't Internet access in the staterooms. He was at ease, full of facts like a museum docent and obviously excited in a way that felt alienating to me. He was looking forward to blending into this world, and all I wanted was to escape it.

Stella's three-year-old daughter used to hide when she saw an aircraft carrier on TV. She thought that it was alive and feeding off the people inside it, and that it ate her dad for months at a time. The weekend we all toured the boat, she seemed to have forgotten this impression and detailed to me her plans to become a helicopter pilot when she was six, and then to take up jets so she could make big noises and land on boats.

Over the course of the weekend, every time we drove over the bridge from San Diego to Coronado Island, she strained in her car seat to ask which boat was her dad's, and every time I pointed to the giant gray mass out in the bottle green water. She seemed reassured by its size and told me nothing in the world could break it, not even monsters. I wished my impressions were as clear and comforting, and I continued to wish that when we came back home and I watched Ross start to pack.

PART II

CHAPTER 9

There was no big good-bye when Ross deployed, no movie star kiss, no tears. Just a silent car ride to the hangar, where I practically shoved him out, and then my satin-sheet-buying trip to Hanford, the marathon cleaning session, and the weeping afterward. We had been saying good-bye for weeks already. Ross said it by rotating the tires on the vehicles, changing the oil, and adding reminders to the calendar for when to fertilize the rosebush and when to take the pets for vaccinations. I said it by buying him a book of stamps and some envelopes and trying not to hover in the doorways while he packed. I attended wives' club meetings that lasted forever as they covered everything from the trivial to the earthshaking—we'll do group care package parties; let's update our wills; how about a weekly pajama party for watching *The Bachelor*; we should get a power of attorney for signatures; let's plan a Halfway Party and go out on the town; OPSEC—here's the code for port schedules (never give it away on Facebook or e-mail!); let's make squadron yard signs! And here it was again, albeit in an updated version that didn't mention bridge club or dancing: the Emergency Data Form. This time it came with a call tree and instructions—in case of an incident one of these people will call you, and *do not speak to the media*. Our worlds, our tasks and priorities, split long before we did.

Stella was an excellent sounding board through all the pre-deployment chaos, but in the first few weeks after the guys left, it was also an incredible relief to have to get in the car for my hour-long commute to Fresno for work and school. The long drive through miles of flat farmland under hazy sky became my dedicated time to go from being the lonely, left-behind wife in a rural town, three states away from her family, to the capable administrative assistant arranging literary readings, logging manuscripts for the poetry book contest, and helping with the yearly writers' conference for local high school students. I had deadlines to meet, essays to write and critique, people to talk to about things I cared about that had absolutely nothing to do with the Navy.

In an attempt to reconcile these two worlds, and try to understand my time apart from Ross without putting one long unbroken GONE line through half of a wall calendar, I bought a four-foot-long linear calendar that accounted for time as a gradual changing of seasons. It was covered with beautifully detailed illustrations of what was going on in the natural world at any given moment, and it even gave each day its own fanciful and unique name to avoid the repetition of Monday, Tuesday, Wednesday, and so on. Weeks, the calendar said, were meaningless man-made concepts. Reframe time, I reasoned, and maybe huge blocks of it spent sleeping alone wouldn't hurt so much.

By this calendar, then, it was "MoonIce," and not just another rainy Thursday morning in January with Ross only two weeks gone, when I dropped an old TV on my foot inside a rusty boxcar used as a recycling facility for broken electronics. Lying on my side in the boxcar, gasping as huge, throbbing bolts of pain shot up my leg, I considered my options. I had my phone on me and I could have called Stella, but it was early and she would have to strap her kids into their car seats to come get me. I would need to figure out some way of getting the foot x-rayed probably, but this seemed like a giant hassle. Far more pressing was the question of how I would drive the truck once I got out of the boxcar. Our old pickup had a stick shift and required the use of my left foot on the clutch. I decided to focus on this hurdle, and then reward myself, if I could successfully drive, by going to Starbucks for some more measured thinking. The two paramedics standing in line ahead of me for coffee seemed like some sort of divine coincidence.

"Excuse me," I said, tapping one on the shoulder. "I hate to bother you, but I was just wondering—if I dropped something on the bridge of my foot but I can still move all my toes, that means it can't be broken, right?"

"Well, that depends. Did you—can I take a look? Is it that foot?"

I still hadn't looked at it. I lifted the cuff of my jeans to expose the angry, swelling lump above my rain-soaked moccasin and immediately regretted it. The paramedic let out a low whistle and started to explain greenstick fractures, but I couldn't hear him because a familiar feeling was taking over. My ears were filling with cotton and my vision had tunneled down to a pinpoint. I held up a finger, unable to talk but meaning, *Excuse me a minute. I need . . . a minute . . . This thing is about to happen again.*

I fainted. Simply saying it like that is misleading, though, because every time I do it—and I've done it far more times than I can count, beginning sometime around the third grade when I keeled over from my first blood test—there's lots more unintentional theater involved. When I faint, I invariably try to fight it, which means I waste precious seconds tensing up instead of getting to the ground, and I end up falling like a cut tree. Once I'm there, likely having taken out either another person or a tray of glass things or food on the way down, I have what's termed a "pseudoseizure," where I convulse for a few seconds with my eyes wide open and rolled into the back of my head, and then I go limp. When I come to, I have no idea where I am for a few minutes and frequently use the time to burst into tears and start apologizing.

Fainting runs in my family, on my mother's side. In my mind's eye I can still see her lying on her back on any number of floors, public and private, with her feet propped up against the wall, her face pale against the sprawl of her curls, waving her hand limply as she reassures everyone around her, "I'm all right, I just feel a little faint." Of all of us, my mother is the only one with sense enough, or perhaps humility, to lie down when she begins to feel like she might faint. "I get to the floor before the floor gets to me," she says. A brief list of places she has lain in recent years: a movie theater, an allergist's office, a florist shop, the oral surgeon's office, and the emergency room (those last two not as patient but as mother of patient—from the ground she offered her hand for me to hold while I came to from wisdom tooth surgery and during repeated attempts to start an IV on me for an appendectomy). People bring her water in these situations and give each other looks.

I *hate* that I faint because everything about the act contradicts an image of myself that I have worked very hard, for a very long time, to cultivate. When I was in elementary school, I started to notice a term cropping up in discussions about me between my mother and various teachers: "high-strung." Other times, trying to sugarcoat it, perhaps, they would use "artistic temperament" or "sensitive." Often, my father's absences and their effect on me were invoked to explain tendencies in my personality, to the point that I finally realized that being singled out for "special conversations" about stress or sadness with my teachers during recess meant that I was an object of pity, someone who wasn't quite handling things. The realization offended me in the same way seeing the stewardesses give me the "I'm sorry" face at the airport did. You think I'm not brave; you think I'm weak. Since then, I have tried everything in my power to cultivate an image of steely, unflappable competence, to appear to the rest of the world to be the exact opposite of someone whose imagination can overreact to injury so much that I literally—and regularly—overrun my own neural circuits and crash twitching to the floor.

"I can't get a radial." John Coltrane's "My Favorite Things" is playing softly in the background. *I had that on CD—where is that CD?* "Move that table. Excuse us, folks, can we get the gurney in here?" The smell of burned coffee, someone tugging at my sweatshirt, trying to pull it over my head. *No! I'm not wearing a shirt underneath!*

"Ma'am? Can you hear me? Are you on any medication for epilepsy? Ma'am?"

"I'm s-so sorryyy . . ." *Oh, my God, oh, shit, that's me. I've fainted again and I sound drunk.*

The faint at the Lemoore Starbucks counted as different from previous ones because it was the first for which I had no obvious backup to come get me, or laugh about yet another addition to my long history of embarrassments. Ross and I had e-mailed sporadically, but an actual phone call was still a month or more away. In order to release me from their impromptu care, the paramedics insisted that I call someone, and when I insisted back that I was fine, they counterinsisted, for liability reasons. Thankfully, a nearby group of women volunteered to take charge of me long enough for my color to return.

The women turned out to be military wives married to enlisted men in the Army, and as I sat there sipping my water, I learned that their husbands were serving out year-long deployments in Iraq. As in, twelve months in a combat zone for a fraction of the pay Ross was getting. And after two weeks with my husband in the Pacific, a tour I'd been hearing derisively referred to as a "booze cruise," there I sat with my swollen foot and thready pulse, willing my hands to stop shaking as a thick bar of sunlight painted the back of my neck and spilled onto my lap and the chairs around me, making everything, including the kind and patient smiles of the women monitoring my color, look thoroughly normal and thoroughly fine. I was the sensitive kid again, the one who couldn't handle it. The women invited me to their evangelical Christian church service the following week, and I wondered briefly if maybe that was the missing piece, a bracing dose of Jesus in my life, but ultimately I finished my water, gushed my profuse thanks and profound embarrassment, and limped back to the truck and my empty house, where I put a bag of frozen peas on my foot and sat down for a good cry.

The most difficult part of the early days of the deployment was this periodic feeling of being vulnerable. Even scarier, though, was the realization that my instincts here, the construction of a front of competency and strategies like toughing it out, were doomed to fail. Stella was offended when I relayed the story to her and showed her the bruise that would have me limping for a week, but would remain otherwise uninvestigated.

"Jesus, what's the matter with you? *Call me.*"

"Don't worry, you're on my boxcar injury speed dial now," I joked, but she didn't laugh. We always kidded, always rolled our eyes at the syrupy lines we heard at the wives' club meetings about leaning on "your Navy family." That was part of what made it okay for her to know how messed up my life really was. That, and my determination that I would not have to lean.

"We're on our own now. You get that, right? We look out for each other." *We're on our own now.* But for the first time since Ross had started leaving, months before the boat actually took him, I felt like that might not be true.

CHAPTER 10

When Ross and I got married, I made a rule: no base living. As much as possible we would live "out in town" wherever we were stationed and work to cultivate a network of nonmilitary friends, a separation of life and work, and a place to be off duty. It was also a way for me to keep the Navy at arm's length and maintain my own identity and sense of privacy. It all seemed like a good idea, and it worked for five years, from the beginning of flight school and up to Lemoore. Then I discovered that we were living across the street from a meth dealer.

Hip-Hop was what Ross and I called him, and he spent his days mostly in his own half-open garage, where he slouched shirtless in a lawn chair, smoking cigarettes and texting for hours at a time. He wore big, white-framed plastic sunglasses and baggy pajama pants with a loud print of electric green surf company logos. Cars came and went in his driveway all day. They pulled in with windows down and subwoofers thumping and, like a grouchy, pimp-limping carhop, he would stroll over and lean against the driver's side, blow a blue jet of smoke up over his shoulder, and chat for a moment. Then he would disappear inside his house and return, lean fully inside the window and punch knuckles with the driver and passengers a couple of times, and then off they would go and he would return to his lawn chair. Other characters lived there too, or rotated in and out—a girl I called Two-Tone for her blond-on-top, black-on-bottom hair color; Bulldog, a bald, mashed-faced guy; and Little Pants, an impossibly skinny guy on the cutting edge of teenage fashion in his breathlessly tight pants. Various toddlers came and went, herded by girls with stringy hair and big jackets. The entire cast was white, and at first it was kind of comical, the seriousness with which he took his avocation in this rural farming town. I told Stella Hip-Hop stories when we drank beers on her back porch after she put her kids to bed.

Out our front windows and across our lawns, Hip-Hop and I stared at the tableau of each other's lives. What he saw was a lawn prone to overgrowth and dandelions; an old blue pickup truck with Texas plates parked in the driveway, its back window covered in Navy fighter squadron stickers; and a garage, when it yawned open late at night, with dusty surfboards and mountain bikes that never came down off their pegs and a crumbling wall of still-packed moving boxes. What he saw was a couple on opposite schedules, a house permanently awake and half empty, the way station we lived in while we waited for the next reassignment.

We didn't like each other, Hip-Hop and I. We were just close enough in age that I hated his music; not for its genre, rap and hip-hop, but his choices within that genre—T.I., for instance, and not Tupac. He watched me stretch for my daily run, and if I were a few years younger I might have mistaken this for him checking out my body, a twisted sort of compliment, instead of the blatant aggression it was. What bugged me about it was that he didn't drop his gaze when I caught him staring and scowled back; his stare was a territorial challenge, and it made me feel like I had less of a right to my place. Also, he invited his buddies to set up lawn chairs to watch and laugh while I attempted to mow and edge the lawn one sunny morning shortly after Ross deployed. They formed a line, the three of them, their white torsos and chicken ribs exposed to the sun, their eyes hidden behind sunglasses. I kept getting tangled up in the rosebush trying to groom the grass beneath it, and I put the wrong gas, the gas mixed with oil for the edger, into the mower, and it began to smoke. I wanted to cry. They cracked open beers.

Mostly, though, we were able to avoid each other. I worked and went to evening classes in Fresno, and he didn't open his garage most mornings until around eleven, so the only times we saw each other were late nights when I came home from school and idled in the street for a few seconds while my garage door lifted, framing a well-lit, wide-angle exposure of my stored life. His half-open door spilled fluorescent light and exposed a card table covered in a forest of red plastic cups, folding chairs, scattered ashtrays, and a child's plastic swimming tub, dusty and propped up on one end. The light lengthened the shadow of him in his chair and caught the puffs of smoke as they drifted above his head. He still wore the shades.

I love the HBO series *The Wire*, and at the time I lived across the street from Hip-Hop, I would go through long stretches where I sacrificed sleep at the end of a sixteen-hour day just to see whether McNulty and Lieutenant Daniels had finally caught up with Avon

Barksdale and Stringer Bell, or that creepy bastard Marlo. I loved the cops, but I loved the dealers too, and I especially loved the ones caught in the middle, like the renegade Omar, who followed his own complicated moral calculus in meting out vengeance among the various dealers. I thought about them when I wasn't watching the show. I wondered about their lives, which direction I would take if circumstances were different and I was in their situation, either protecting a corner or trying to crack a drug ring.

This was what I was doing home alone one Friday night, a month after fracturing my foot and fainting in Starbucks, thinking about plot machinations on *The Wire* after watching three episodes back-to-back on DVD. I had just turned off the TV and was heading to bed when four explosions, the biggest firecrackers I'd ever heard, went off in front of my house. I felt the percussions in my chest and heard the windows rattle in their frames, and before I even knew what I was doing, I was on my knees in the living room, crawling fast toward the kitchen wall to reach up and turn off the light switch. Gunshots. They were gunshots.

I dragged my purse down from the kitchen table, dug out my phone, and dialed 911. I got a recording that said something ridiculous like, "Nine-one-one Emergency, please hold for an available operator. Thank you." On hold, I watched the red glow of taillights move slowly across the ceiling through the wide-open curtains in my living room. The lights passed, and then a brighter version, the added whites of a car in reverse, came back again. I held my breath and crawled out into the living room, both wishing I was staying put and knowing I could get a glimpse of the car that might help the cops. I peeked quickly, once, and saw a beat-up white Neon, and as I ducked back down I heard its engine whine as it raced off down the street.

Finally, the 911 operator came on. I gave her my address and told her what had happened. She asked if I knew what kind of gun was used, and I made a guess—a handgun for sure because I knew what my grandfather's hunting rifles and shotguns sounded like and it wasn't that, and possibly a .45 for the bigger explosion instead of the pop of a nine-millimeter. Ross's buddy, a former Marine, had taken us target shooting once on a camping trip and I had been prepared to hate the collection of handguns he laid out, had even planned on using the experience as the basis for an antigun essay, but then discovered that I was an excellent shot, and preferred the stronger kick and noise of the .45. I have felt shamefully thrilled around guns ever since, a weird mix of a gun control supporter's revulsion and an enthusiast's attraction I can't quite sort out.

The cops were there within minutes. The ceiling in my still-dark house flashed red-white-blue, red-white-blue. They blocked either end of the street and spent the next two and a half hours walking around with their Maglites looking for bullet casings. They inspected every little bit of trash in the gutters, and then they walked through my yard and Hip-Hop's yard, flashing their lights along the outside walls and the windows and behind the bushes.

I didn't go outside. I closed my curtains and kept my lights off and I stood at the very edge of my living room window in the corner where I could see through a half-inch space between the curtain and the wall. I made sure no light touched me, but I made sure I had an unobstructed view. I wanted to help, I wanted to know what had happened, but I also didn't want to tell anyone that Ross was deployed, that I was alone and would be for the next five months.

There was a party in progress at Hip-Hop's that night and everyone spilled out onto the front lawn. He gestured wildly and darted around between cops and a little knot of partygoers gathered off to one side, smoking and texting and arguing with each other. Every time a cop approached the front door, Hip-Hop headed him off. A girl with a ponytail screamed at someone on her phone and then stomped out to the street, where one of the cops had found a bullet hole in the back window of her car. The hole was small and neat. A few of my other neighbors came out to stand awkwardly in the street, talking to cops with notepads. José, a small-engine mechanic who lived next door to me and worked out of his backyard, and Mr. Enriquez, who tended a large menagerie of concrete yard animals, came out to talk, but Hip-Hop hovered within earshot and the conversations were short.

Eventually, another cop found a bullet casing in the front yard and a halfhearted cheer went up in the crowd. The cop marked the spot by picking up a child's orange sand bucket from the flower bed and turning it upside down over the casing. Four bullet holes were found and noted: two in Hip-Hop's kitchen wall, one through the wall in his living room, and one in the back window of the car parked out front. I bit through the last of my fingernails and went to bed, feeling my way in the dark.

I wondered if this brush with danger and the law would chasten Hip-Hop. Maybe things would quiet down. The night after the shooting, Hip-Hop and his buddies were up welding something until dawn, the lightning stutter of spark-light flashing around the edges of the closed garage door, and then an epic party started that lasted for three days. Everyone parked only on my side of the street, and trucks raced up and down the block, letting their after-market mufflers rattle all the car alarms awake.

Stella and I agreed that if anything felt wrong when I came home from work at night, I could go spend the night at her house, a place she and Jake had bought that was only a couple of miles from me, but in a nicer neighborhood.

I thought of *The Wire*'s plot lines of retribution, how Avon Barksdale spent days "tooling up" and organizing a hit back when a competing drug network murdered two of his corner boys, knowing his credibility and reputation were at stake if he let it slide. I kept telling myself this situation was different, it was no big deal, this was rural California, for God's sake, not Baltimore, but I also stopped sleeping.

I didn't want to e-mail all of this to Ross and worry him if there was nothing he could do. But when I had gone by the police station later to ask about the shooting and give a description of the car I saw, I had asked the cop if he thought things would quiet down. He'd simply said, "There are other places to live." For the first time, I considered base living.

Naval Air Station Lemoore shares a zip code with Lemoore proper, but for noise abatement reasons, the base sits about ten miles to the west of town. The Navy leases the surrounding fields to farmers who grow tomatoes and alfalfa and cotton. "Main Side" is where all of the housing and administrative offices are located, as well as the commissary and the Navy Exchange, the gym, the hospital, two elementary schools, and a bunch of different community centers. "Ops Side" is for the airstrips, the hangars, the weapons bunkers, and the shooting ranges. Both sides are guarded by checkpoints where you must stop and show ID, which I did on the morning I went and spoke to Ross's commanding officer's wife at her house on base. She had access on the special phone line only skippers are allowed, and I wanted Ross's advice on whether I should break the lease and move somewhere else. The skipper passed the message on to Ross, who called me back the next day.

"I think you should move on base."

"Yeah, maybe." I hedged. "But the cops know about this guy now. He'll be on their radar."

"That's not exactly comforting when I'm this far away."

"It's just—I don't want to give up our privacy. I don't want to live behind a guarded fence again." What I couldn't bring myself to say was that the last time I had lived on a compound was the year I spent with my family in Saudi Arabia, a year that led to my unraveling. I missed the sound of his voice. The few times my dad had called home from work he'd at least had the grace to sound as far away as he was. It felt cruel, having such a clear phone connection, and wasting precious conversation time on the question of Hip-Hop and whether or not I would agree to move. I visualized a meter like the ones at gas stations, the slower side ticking off the seconds and the faster one calculating how much money it was costing the U.S. government to connect us for this brief moment.

"This is not going to be like Saudi Arabia was for you." Ross was able to hear my unspoken fears. "Please, I need you to do this."

It was a long pause before I said, "Okay."

CHAPTER 11

The Aramco compound in Dhahran, Saudi Arabia, was surrounded by a razor wire fence, and its two gates were manned by Arab guards carrying machine guns and checking IDs. They ran a stick with a mirror on the end along the undersides of vehicles, and when the weather dropped below sixty degrees in the winter, they wore heavy jackets, hats, and gloves. They never looked happy to see us.

"Where iss your EYE-dee? Bedge number!" As a teenager, I was often barked at by compound security guards for looking like I was up to no good, which usually meant being outside my house, and sometimes even being outside my house with a group that included boys. All of us would have to produce our company dependent IDs and recite our fathers' badge numbers, after which it was expected that we move on to sit around somewhere else.

My ID showed a girl with long dark hair, staring wide-eyed and stiff-shouldered into the camera and refusing to smile. The men taking the picture had just finished fingerprinting me, one of them cradling my forearm and stroking its inside as my mother and brother were herded out of the room to wash the ink off their hands. The men had smiled and laughed, told jokes in Arabic while they fluffed my hair in front of my shoulders and steered me into place in front of the camera. Right before the flash, the photographer pursed his lips and made a loud, sucking kiss noise at me. The shock captured in that picture never really wore off for the year I lived there. The whole thing, how I was suddenly turning from a child to a teenager and how we simultaneously ended up in the Middle East, just never stopped being a surprise.

My dad got laid off from his job when I was entering the seventh grade, right after we'd finished building a house in Georgetown, a small town thirty miles north of Austin. The plan had been to move to a place where we could afford a better quality of life. Instead our family spent the next year and a half eating through savings and cashing in my parents' retirement accounts as my dad sent out dozens of resumes a week and my mom just barely floated us on a high school math teacher's salary. They fought and worried and fought some more, and my dad's depression went from chronic and long-simmering into something darker, something that spurred my mom to hide his shotguns in the back of the attic. I grew from an awkward kid into an awkward teenager, channeling all the angst I felt over my disintegrating home life into playing the clarinet in the junior high honor band. Then my dad took us all out for dinner one night and dropped a bomb. We were moving to Saudi Arabia.

Dad fiddled with the salt and pepper shakers and spoke gravely and at length about the sacrifices he would need from us to assure our family's future. It was the tail end of my eighth grade year and my brother's seventh grade one. Dad would leave almost immediately. Mom would stay behind with me and Doug until we finished the school year, at which point we would pack up most of our furniture into long-term storage and rent out the home we'd just built to strangers. I had no way of knowing it at the time, but starting with the move to Georgetown, and for the rest of my life up to now, I would never again live in one place for more than three years at a stretch.

Ladies and gentlemen, we will be entering the airspace of the Kingdom of Saudi Arabia in thirty minutes." The pilot's announcement, repeated at twenty minutes and again at ten, was evidently a countdown for last call with the drink carts, and also a cue for the Muslim women aboard to disappear into the airplane bathrooms and reemerge covered from head to toe in black veils, head scarves, *abayas*, and in some cases gloves. As the seats filled up with black and the plane began its descent, what had been a fairly chatty flight grew quiet. I remember a balding British man who got so drunk on the flight that as soon as we walked down the rolling staircase to the tarmac, oven hot even at night, he had to sit on his luggage and scoot forward while we waited in a long line to enter the airport building. *What is the matter with him?* I wondered. This was before we walked through a blast of cold, cigarette-smelling air into Dhahran Airport, and into a sea of men, all pressed together for the hours-long wait at customs. They were laborers fresh off jumbo jets from India, Bangladesh, and Sri Lanka, and what I noticed, apart from how skinny they all were, was how much everyone stared at the small group of exposed Western women coming off our flight.

It had been mentioned in our cultural orientation in Houston, a week before we flew out, that men in the Middle East had a different way of interacting with women. This was said in the kind of offhand, casual way that one would note that the desert is hot. It was not considered rude to stare, said the smiling, pant-suited woman in charge of the seminar for children, in which my brother and I were the only teenagers. Certain places, stores, or restaurants did not allow women, but sometimes there would be a sign on the door pointing to an alternate entrance and a smaller, screened-off "family" section. Then she singled out me and my pasty Irish complexion and said, "And what a lovely tan *you'll* get!" So I was unprepared, to say the least, for how unnerving the stares felt coming from every corner, how threatening and all en-compassing. When we finally got through customs to my dad, now darkly tanned, twenty pounds lighter, and grinning like a maniac, I ran up and hugged him with a magnetic appeal for the shadow of his protection, something I hadn't felt I needed, or that he could provide, since I was a little kid. *Hide me.*

The Aramco compound, at first glance, seemed to me much like a middle-class American suburb except that the signs were in English and Arabic. Our house, number 150 on the corner of First and Gazelle, was on a part of the compound called Main Camp. The houses, identical and arranged close together with circuit board regularity, were called modulars. Different jobs within the company carried different "grade codes," a sort of ranking system that determined not only salary but also where you were allowed to live. Families with higher grade codes, or those with accrued seniority, could live in "the Hills," where the houses were larger and varied and the yards had trees.

Our modular had a sunny yellow exterior, a red front door, and a little postage stamp yard, which nevertheless came with the weekly services of a Nepalese gardener. Inside, the walls were stark white and the banged-up company-issued furniture a muted brown. My dad had stockpiled a few groceries, and once Doug and I settled whose room was whose, I retreated to mine with a pruney tasting Arabic Dr Pepper, jet-lagged but awake for most of the night, and began to unpack. It was the early morning call to prayer, a rising and falling song along a double harmonic scale, blasting over loudspeakers from a nearby mosque, that broke through my stupor. The sun was rising already at nearly four a.m., and as I listened at my bedroom window, opened to the strange smells of smoke and dust in the gray morning sky, other mosques chimed in and the air seemed momentarily full of voices echoing the same call with variations.

The various prayer calls would eventually become a deeply felt sensory memory for me, neither wholly positive nor wholly negative. I soon learned to identify my favorite prayer callers, or muezzins. Hearing one in the movies now as part of the cinematic shorthand Hollywood uses to indicate *foreign!* brings back the smell of hot asphalt and oil refineries, and the faint notes of open sewage and salt water from the nearby Gulf. It brings back the feeling of midday heat so intense that the pores on my face would tighten when I opened the front door as if I were opening the door of an oven, and nights that were never truly quiet or dark, and instead a hazy amber from the streetlights in the dusty air, which obscured the stars. It brings back the anxiety I felt wandering the lost-in-translation shops of downtown al-Khobar (the Decent Barber, the Fondled Child) and al-Shula Mall, which was continually under construction, with the dusty hulks of gutted escalators piled in the dirt parking lot. I remember the American servicemen in desert camo and the continual background noise from the Dhahran air base, at the time a temporary home for American Air Force jets enforcing the no-fly zone over Iraq.

We arrived in 1993, two years after the official end of the Persian Gulf War. Three years later we moved back to the United States, leaving my dad temporarily behind in Saudi Arabia and looking for a job again, this time so he could come back and join us. He found one, but not before being jolted awake one night by the Khobar Towers bombing, the explosion knocking framed pictures from the walls of the living room.

And then after I remember these things, I remember what I felt for most of the short time I lived there—a sense of bewildered imbalance that came from repeatedly being unable to see what was coming, and the impression that no matter what the company or my new friends said, we were not supposed to be there, both "we" in the larger sense as Westerners and "we" in the particular: my family, and especially, I thought, *me.*

I got my first period two days after stepping off the plane in Dhahran and bought my first jumbo box of maxipads from an Arab man at the company commissary who wouldn't touch the box and instead nudged it across the scanner with his pen, and who then made me lay my riyals on the counter, where he gingerly pinched them up instead of taking them from my hand. I both loved and hated getting off the compound for trips to the Arab Safeway or one of the malls because it meant I was exchanging one kind of scrutiny—that of a stimulus-deprived expatriate community—for another, the broader community of Saudis and Filipinos and day laborers from all over Southeast Asia. The first was benign, mostly confirming over and over again that I was new in town; the second was more interesting but ran the risk of turning hostile. I never got tired of seeing little kids finding their veiled moms in the supermarket by their outrageously flashy shoes, or watching old men unroll their prayer rugs on the crusty edges of the beach, facing east and summoning inner quiet amid all the honking car horns. But weighed against that was the time I was cornered in an antique shop by a Saudi man who shoved his hand deep between my legs and squeezed, or the time a pack of teenage Arab boys at a dilapidated roadside carnival chased me and a pack of girlfriends across a dark parking lot as we ran for the last evening Aramco bus back to the compound.

Ninth grade was the last year of schooling available for the children of foreign workers in Saudi Arabia. After that, companies paid to ship the kids off to boarding schools of the families' choosing, anywhere in the world. I was still trying to come to terms with the fact that I would be leaving home (such as it was) at fifteen, and I had no idea where I wanted to go. My classmates, who were militantly competitive about who had gotten the latest Primus T-shirt airmailed from a friend back in "the States," and who got to vacation in Kenya or Switzerland over their families' "repat" travel breaks, already knew where they wanted to go, and the fact that I had no clue what each school name meant in terms of its placement along the scale of academic elitism or hard partying was only further evidence that even though I was the freshest import, I was so behind the times. A friend had to pull me aside after I'd been "going with" a boy named Jad for two weeks to ask pointedly if I knew what "frigid" meant, and how the word was being applied to me. I had to answer that no, in fact, I didn't know what it meant, that in this country that topped out daily at 120 degrees, I'd been singled out as frigid.

I was one of three new kids in my ninth grade class of seventy-five, and pretty much every day felt like being a turtle getting pried out of its shell. There seemed to be only two currents to follow socially. You could be a good kid and attend the weekly church groups, renamed "morale meetings," and find favor among the few well-connected families who had memberships to the Mission Inn, a former military mess hall where you could get root beer and sometimes even bacon; or you could be a bad kid and hang out with the older "returning students" back from boarding school for holiday visits, drinking the home-brewed alcohol everyone called *sidiki* (Arabic for "friend"), smoking Afghani hash, and getting it on. Like in any small town, rumor was a powerful force, and it hardly mattered whether you actually did any, or all, or some combination of these things; it just mattered what you were *perceived* and *reported* to be doing.

I had a fuzzy perception of my reputation among my peers, enough to understand that I was a disappointment as a girlfriend and a source of perplexed annoyance among the pack of girls that eventually claimed me. The only relationship I had that hung on past the tumult of high school, and within which I felt something closest to my true self, was with my friend Larry, another relatively recent import. We both lived on Main Camp and walked together to and from school and passed notes in English class, and with his strict Chinese mom and white, ex-military dad, Larry alone seemed subject to the same frequent groundings as me, the same stern lectures, and the same as-yet-unfounded parental suspicions. In other words, his family seemed about as uncomfortable in Saudi Arabia, for whatever reason, as mine.

There was a prom and a graduation ceremony and then some kind of big, beach-based good-bye party, but I attended none of these. As soon as our required residency year in-kingdom was up, my mom had the whole family on a flight to Scotland to make the most of our remaining time together before I got jettisoned to boarding school back in the United States. I was already out of the country before I understood I could never really go back to Saudi Arabia again for anything other than a short visit. Even if my parents had stayed longer and sent both Doug and me through boarding school and on to college, once we reached twenty-five, we would be among all the other children of foreign workers who had aged out of their access to the kingdom. Even if that was your childhood home—and for many of my classmates, it was—its doors closed to you forever. Unless you repeated the whole cycle by going to work for Aramco, a pattern that was not uncommon. Remembering the various versions of expat life in Saudi Arabia, a practice to which whole Web-based forums and Facebook pages are devoted, takes on the peculiar quality of hypernostalgia. There is a premium placed on how thoroughly you can remember, how long you spent there, how much you belonged to that life. (Doug, incidentally, adjusted much better to life in the desert, enough to remember it fondly. Whether this is because of the few additional freedoms allowed to boys or because he's just fundamentally more adaptable than me, I don't know.)

But we didn't stay. We didn't belong. I can't claim to be a "Saudi kid" or an "Aramco brat" because I'm not one. I don't qualify—not then, and not now, when there are extended videos on YouTube from the point of view of a handheld camera in the front seat of a car as it drives slowly around the compound in Dhahran as sad piano music plays in the background. I understand the feeling of homesickness, of feeling unmoored in the world with little or no remaining connection to your own history. That feeling for me has only amplified over the years with each successive move, but Saudi Arabia is not a place with any claim on me, or me on it. I consider my time there something close to trespassing —in someone else's country and in someone else's memories of home.

The feeling of not belonging makes me hesitant to claim the Navy as my community now, though every day it becomes clearer to me that the military is a tribe with its own language, its own traditions of including and initiating, separating and grieving, celebrating and always moving on.

CHAPTER 12

Ross and I existed as a couple through the deployment by the grace of our e-mail correspondence. Compressed into online identities, fooled, perhaps, by the illusion of instantaneous contact over the ether, we became an affectionate cybercouple creative in the ways we addressed each other (McManpants, Ladyface, Sexy Von Sassyboots), but then mostly lapsing into a crushingly boring blow-by-blow of our financial situation. There was a lot to talk about—our dog's dubious emergency X-rays, the mystery warning lights on my car, our unexpected household move, Ross's budget for souvenirs and requests for stuff to include in the next care package, how to file the taxes. Ross was writing from the only place he had Internet access, the ready room, and I felt like I was always talking to his public, at-work side; I wrote from the white-walled silence of our house on base. Our missives, preserved for posterity by Google, would make excellent court documents but really, really dull romance.

During brief port calls, I watched Facebook light up with

veiled notifications (Code words! No locations! OPSEC!) from the other wives that the guys were ashore and could now call home, which felt like some kind of weird competition about who would get called first. When Ross skipped a phone call opportunity completely in Japan, I was heartbroken. Incidentally, no correct response exists to another wife's complaints about her contact with her husband during a deployment. "Oh, I'm sorry" in response to "No, he didn't call from Japan" feels like confirmation that an unforgivable breach of trust has occurred. "Eh, maybe next time; I'm sure it was hard to get a moment," on the other hand, feels like denial that it hurts or is even important. Relating to the other wives throughout cruise was like being in a dark room where we felt our way around by swinging baseball bats. Everyone's cruise, whether it was their fifth or their first, was completely different, and often without meaning to, we ended up smacking each other in the face with well-intentioned but completely inappropriate comments.

Male-deprivation sickness set in. I began to harbor completely inappropriate random crushes, fictional ones that took place entirely in my own head but nonetheless interfered wildly with my emotional thermostat. I felt like a threat to the general population, like my untended need for the simplest bodily sensations of maleness—the smell of aftershave, rough hands, shoulders set above mine—was prying at the hinges of my sanity. I felt like I was growing fangs.

Throughout it all, I had a growing suspicion that Ross was having an okay time. He didn't miss me, or at least, not to the same extent. I pictured myself on the little shelf by his bed, safely compartmentalized and set aside, our life together shelved and bookmarked and available for periodic reengagement in the rare moments when nothing else required his attention. I couldn't have articulated any of this, but the feeling of smallness, the feeling of great and impossible distance and an unbridgeable gulf between us, smoldered in me.

In April, just past the halfway point, a port call, the Holy Grail of deployments, popped up and glittered on the horizon. Singapore. Could we afford it? Ross and I weighed the financial hit against the ever-present possibility that the carrier would reschedule at the last minute, scrapping some or all of our brief reunion, but we decided to go for it. Stella and Jake did too. The next couple of weeks passed in a giddy blur of trip planning, Stella and I poring over guidebooks together and seeking out food recommendations from an episode of Anthony Bourdain's *No Reservations*. She had her mom come stay with the kids and I arranged for time off work and boarded my pets. We flew out of San Francisco and over the Pacific with vodka tonics in hand and surgical masks over our faces given the bird flu epidemic. "To us, Roxy," Stella toasted, using what she had termed my "bad girl" name. "To all the limes that gave their lives for our caipirinhas," I added, "and to your garbage disposal, may it rest in peace." It was easy and fun, joking about our overenthusiastic drinking and all the nights we'd spent bullshitting on her back porch after her kids were asleep. It was also a far less painful way to cross international borders than being dragged along as a miserable teenager, but as Ross and I drew nearer to each other on the globe, I felt my heart drawing back and an unexpected anger rising up.

By the time the guys met us in the lobby of our towering glass hotel in downtown Singapore, Stella was nervously sneaking a cigarette and I was a precariously balanced sculpture of crazy, all porcelain and knives and nitroglycerin. For the first forty-eight hours, Ross was a startlingly lifelike cardboard rendition of himself. For years I'd been hearing tales from other wives of steamy reunions in exotic locales, that it was the best part of a cruise and great for keeping the spark alive. The dissonance between their stories and my current reality I took as evidence of what I already suspected: something was wrong with me, or with us, and I wasn't doing any of this right.

I tried to find solace in the subway on our first night together. I loved the announcement wording on the MRT, Singapore's public transport, recorded by a woman with a kind British accent and then played on a digital screen in English, Chinese, and what I later learned were Malay and Tamil: "Next station, Dhoby Ghaut. Passengers continuing their journey on the North East Line, please alight." Their journey. Please alight. Like birds on migration. And it was that orderly. Everyone stood around texting, not shouting into their phones. Indian mamas drowsed next to their big-eyed children in the gentle shaking of the tunnels. We could go anywhere with our little green transit card, tapping our way in and out of electronic turnstiles and flowing along in the air-conditioned veins underneath the city with orange-robed Buddhist monks shuffling along next to us with iPod headphones plugged into their ears. I felt like part of the big humming blood of something, and that wherever I got on or off, it would be the right place. It was all new, in other words, novel, strange, miraculous, *not* the Central Valley of California and the overdue oil change, chaotic checkbook register, and flat Highway 41 whose sixty-five-mile stretch of dairy farms and raisin fields I'd been traversing alone for months on end. Singapore was fascinating and a deep relief to the feeling of being stuck. But being back together with Ross, the part I'd expected to feel like quenching a long-held thirst, instead felt scary—awkward and delicate, like at any moment he could just disappear again without warning.

In silent moments across plates of strange food, I tried to see myself as he saw me, and I realized I had deliberately changed the view. My hair was even shorter, too short probably, and I'd decided against all logic and prior habit to get French-tipped acrylic nails that made it hard to zip my own pants or put in my contacts. I had lost ten pounds. Back in California I'd managed to think that these were improvements I was making to surprise him, but as we spent more time alone together I remembered how he'd always liked my hair longer, that he hated fake nails, that he liked me at a more athletic weight. I also knew that I looked tired and couldn't keep still, that I was draining my drinks a little too quickly and he was noticing, and that we kept missing each other's hands or arms when we tried to embrace or reach out. I had changed the view, and part of me realized what I wanted to say by doing it: *You haven't been here.* How is it possible to miss someone so much and then be covered in spikes when you finally see them again?

I don't remember what we said when we finally got around to talking about it. I remember we were lying on our sides on the hotel bed, facing each other but at opposite ends like a pair of open parentheses not sure of what was between them, his head by my knees, my head by his, twenty-three floors above street level with the patio door open to the humid breeze and the distant shouts of cricket players below. *I don't understand where this is coming from—why are you so upset?* At various points, one or both of us would break the parentheses to flop on our backs and stare in frustration at the ceiling. *Don't you get it? That's the problem. We're living completely separate lives.* I didn't know how to explain to him how enraged I felt to see him flip on the little "Rachel" switch in his mental cockpit, as if the intervening months of separation had been no big deal. I felt mangled by the deployment, aged and withered by the grind of time alone, going nowhere, while he seemed to be aging in reverse, periodically infused with new life by adventures like holding an actual tiger cub at the Thailand Zoo or going to a baseball game in Japan. Usually when we argue I cry like a quiet leaking—no actual sobs or quavering voice, just a long, repetitive series of sniffles. But in Singapore, voicing the feeling that had been building in me—*I can't do this anymore*—I couldn't cry. I thought about punching the walls or jumping off the balcony or smashing the bottle of wine we'd bought at the corner store, but that was only briefly and at the beginning of the conversation when we could still turn back. Ross scrubbed his face with both palms open and slid his fingers down over his mouth and held them there. *I don't know how to fix this. I don't even know what's broken.*

With an open mess between us, Ross and I agreed to call a truce. We worked on finding each other's hands again as we wandered through Buddhist temples and dodged into tiny shops and under awnings amid the pounding midday tropical thunderstorms. We took refuge often in the sheltering presence of Jake and Stella, the four of us picking up a more familiar rhythm, each with a friend around to act as translator. Stella understood the things I couldn't say—the sustained loneliness and craving for intimacy, the maddening sameness of a home that felt temporary and unreal. Jake corroborated the pent-up stories of squadron drama Ross had been hesitant to lay out over e-mail with his colleagues milling around right behind him in the ready room. I helped minimize Stella's household disasters—a broken oven, a pool gone green and buggy, and then a subsequent accidental flooding of the backyard trying to drain and clean said pool—to keep Jake from getting upset or worrying. Instead, I talked about what the kids were up to, how adorable they were. Ross added calming words of encouragement about how easy it would be to fix the household things once he and Jake got back.

By the time we had to say good-bye, I felt like I had just barely opened my heart up again—enough to make it hurt when the duffel bag came back out and swallowed up what small touches of Ross the hotel room held.

"Only three more months," he said. "We can do this." But his eyes held mine like a question until I answered back, "We can do this."

Back in the valley, I picked up the blunt tool of e-mail once again.

"I'm fucking sick of this deployment and the wives' club is driving me crazy."

DELETE.

"I miss you so much I almost don't miss you anymore because I'm so tired of missing you."

DELETE.

"I'm not who I was when you left."

DELETE.

I spent those last three months unpacking and arranging the house while simultaneously cramming my unresolved resentment and loneliness into the back corner of my mind. I was both emotionally numb and in constant motion, preparing for something utterly foreign and built on fantasy, guesswork, and rumor: the fly-in.

When a squadron comes home, it does it with flair. A giant formation flight rakes over the base in a deafening roar, and to meet it, there are handmade signs up and down the main residential roads, yellow ribbons on all the palm trees, and individual welcome banners on the houses. The inside of our hangar was draped in the biggest American flag I had ever seen, probably twenty-five yards long, and local news crews competed with private photographers hired by the wives to capture shots of the reuniting couples and families. It happened on a Friday, the day before the Fourth of July, which made for a double dose of patriotism and local news coverage.

I had helped decorate the hangar the night before with the wives' club and hung giant squadron-themed banners, which took just enough time to confirm that they were all as tired and on edge as me. I'd painted a sign—"Welcome Home!"—and hung it on our garage door. I'd gotten a new dress, restocked the refrigerator, and washed the dog and the vehicles, but I hadn't hired a photographer or invited any family out. So much of our reunion felt uncertain to me—would he be mad at how much of our old stuff I'd thrown away in the sudden move, or how badly I'd messed up the checkbook register and the taxes? What if I couldn't shake the awkwardness and anger I'd felt in Singapore? I didn't want anybody around taking pictures of this experiment if it might be doomed to blow up.

On the morning of the fly-in, I felt dangerously unaccompanied. Two big buckets of hand-sized American flags sat on a table next to hand-frosted jet-shaped cookies. I grabbed a flag to have something to fidget with. All the little kids were dressed in red, white, and blue. With no parents or in-laws to wrangle, and no little kid to bounce on my hip or to yell at to watch where he poked that flag, I felt like an unbalanced equation, like I shouldn't be there at all. Instead, I stood around and tried to smile like this was the most natural thing in the world, spending a morning all dolled up in an overdecorated jet hangar and waiting for my husband, who had morphed into a weird abstraction of longing, to roar home after six months of being gone.

Someone called my name from across the hangar and I was asked if I spoke Spanish. I said sure, thinking a relative needed directions where to park, but instead I came face-to-face with a beautiful reporter in lavender and pink with her shoulder-length black hair flipped up at the ends. She asked if she could interview me for Univision, and I said sure, this time a little more hesitantly. Mine is simple, present-tense, statement-of-fact Spanish, like "The weather is nice," or "Damn, these are good tacos," not nuanced, thoughtful Spanish capable of reflection and prediction. It's ironic, perhaps, but the grammatical tense in which my mind naturally rests, the subjunctive tense of possibility and wish and longing, is the exact tense I can't seem to master in Spanish.

She set me up in front of a cameraman, who adjusted his camera for "white values," which he claimed had to do with using the flag as a backdrop and not having the white come off as blue, but I smiled and imagined a "gringa" knob on the camera that he was torquing up to "high." He needed it—the beautiful reporter's questions were met with tense, staccato answers.

"What are you waiting for today?"

"My husband comes home after six months on a boat."

"How do you feel?"

"Happy. Nervous."

"What have you been doing to prepare?" She had to ask this one again in English.

"Um, clean, clean, clean." I tried furiously to conjugate verbs for "I haven't cooked real food in six months," but it didn't come. Instead I gave a constipated smile and shrug.

"Has anything changed since he's been gone?"

"Yes, um, I move house because of a, um"—in English: "drive-by shooting"—"so it's a new house. He doesn't know where."

Her eyes widened and she dropped the smile for a second to say, "Wow, really?" Then: "Is this is a new dress today?"

"Yes, a new dress." I felt like the idiot I must have sounded like and wondered if this was the curse of being a Navy wife—the only chance you get to explain yourself and it has to be in a foreign language in three-inch heels in front of the world's biggest flag. They turned off the camera and my IQ immediately bounced back up. I gushed promises to her that I did once speak Spanish, long ago, but that my husband speaks much, much more fluently. She said they would come find him when he landed.

The flyover itself was geometrically beautiful, a twelve-plane formation shaped like a broad arrow, like a kite I had when I was little. I knew which plane was Ross's. It appeared not to move at all, just to grow bigger and louder on the horizon, part of a frozen hieroglyphic against the mild blue of the morning sky. It was over in seconds. They swept over us in a wave of noise and before I realized it, I had started to cry. It wasn't the flags or the decorations or all the families, it wasn't the stress and the fatigue of waiting, and it wasn't really even the anticipation of seeing him again and having him next to me. It was that awful and wonderful gap between who we were on the ground and this bigger, scarier, completely mysterious thing he becomes up in the air.

After all this time, it still amazed me that it was actually him up there flying that thing. All the years of studying, practicing, rehearsing, and then this reality? I still felt like I was missing a step. That's him? This is me? This is our life?

When I snapped out of it, I realized the Univision cameraman was only a few feet from me and was filming again. I flicked tears off my cheeks and looked around for someone to talk to but I recognized no one. I watched for jet 112, the one I'd been told was Ross's, but it was near the end. Finally, 112 came around the bend and I could see his helmet there in the cockpit and him waving and I raised my hands and waved back, the little flag going with them, and my eyes tearing up again, seven years old and back at the gates at Robert Mueller Municipal Airport, my heart splitting wide open in front of everyone and nowhere to hide while it all poured out. *Come back to me, come back to me, don't leave me again.* And then the Univision camera was there, right in my line of sight, and I didn't want to ruin the guy's shot, but I felt myself starting to scowl and crane my neck and mouth the word "mother-*fucker.*"

Someone had decided that all the pilots would sit in their cockpits and wait until the last plane came around and parked, and then they would get out, gather up, form a big horizontal line, and walk toward us. This last little choreographed delay infuriated me, but I tried to keep it from my face. I didn't want scenes from *Top Gun*, I didn't want our every reaction documented for all time in soft focus and framed by the overbearing presence of the flag, and I didn't want this pressure to re-create the sailor/nurse kiss from *Life* magazine, to keep eking out that Good War nostalgia from a time and circumstance where it didn't fit. Most of all, I didn't know how I was supposed to do this, how I was supposed to bring him back to me after this hole had opened up between us, and I didn't want anyone watching while I tried. I just wanted him home. Ross. The guy who made up dirty lyrics to radio songs and left his shoes in the middle of the floor.

The whirring and clicking and beeping of cameras grew louder as the jets' engines spooled down. When the squadron finally started its walk toward us, all lined up in their special matching black flight suits, the crowd surged forward and people waiting in the hangar broke into a run. Wives in heels tried to manage the run holding little kids' hands. The camera crews ran too, dragging cables and backpedaling and trying to get planted for the big reunion kiss shot.

I walked. I couldn't find him at first among all the identical flight suits. A mother clipped me as she ran past, and there was a lightning second where I wondered if this would be like musical chairs and the song would stop without me finding him and I'd be left alone out there on the windy tarmac. And then I saw him. He was farther apart at the very end of the line, laughing. He had seen me the whole way and he was walking too. We slowed down for a minute, even paused. More people ran between us.

When I got to him the collision was slow but I gripped him tighter and tighter and it was like everything else finally stopped for a minute—all the noise, all the people and cameras—and it was just a sunny day and he was home and I could cry and no one was watching. It was a long time before I realized I hadn't even said anything to him yet. When I pulled back, he handed me a rose with a black and red bow on its stem—all the pilots had one—and what I noticed was, *No thorns; someone cut off the thorns?*

The beautiful reporter waited a polite interval before she came up and pointed a microphone at him, and he reacted with grace and poise, stitching together long, melodious Spanish sentences about how fantastic it was to see me again after such a long time. She asked him what he would say to other service members who were away from their families, and he advised patience and faith and said the reunion was better than anything and made everything that came before worth it. I think we were all a little stunned, the reporter, the cameraman, and me. She seemed genuinely dazzled and told him his Spanish was beautiful and that we'd be on at six.

There were a lot of scheduled social events with the squadron that felt like supervised tutorials in how to enjoy being back together, and the unfortunate truth was that we needed them. We sat across from each other at parties, Stella and I with our own language and inside jokes, Ross and Jake with theirs, and a strange gulf between us all now that we were on home turf. In the coming days, Ross was adrift in the new house, frequently asking where things were and being met with the reply, "I'm not sure." Outwardly innocent exchanges between the two of us nevertheless seemed to carry the same undertones—I ferreted out what I interpreted as criticisms of how I'd handled things alone for six months; he fired back from what he heard as attacks for being gone in the first place. In the blank white kitchen, in the box-filled garage, in our half-dark bedroom under strips of streetlight slicing through the blinds and over the constant rumble of jet noise, we fought. He was suddenly everywhere, it seemed, and it was unnerving. I zipped from the bathroom to the closet after showering, my towel wrapped so tightly around me it stung the skin under my arms.

The base house had three bedrooms, enough for us both to

claim a study if we gave up the idea of a dedicated guest room. We retreated to our separate studies often. His view was of our tiny backyard full of gopher mounds. Mine was of the front corner of our neighbors' house. The other strange thing about living on base was that everywhere I looked, I saw alternate versions of Ross and me. No old people for neighbors, no civilians, just pilots, pilots everywhere. Rob and Lily, the neighbors, had a rosebush out front and a forest of potted plants along the edges of their back fence, and bamboo wind chimes that bonked and clacked in the breeze at night and made it sound like a real neighborhood. Two cushioned chairs sat on either side of their front door, and in the mornings when the weather was nice, they would sit out there and have coffee together. Our front porch had a potted geranium, which stubbornly refused to die despite my neglect, and a broom for whacking at black widow nests. Ostensibly writing, I spent long hours sitting in my study wondering how much room a crib would take up and if I would ever have a need to find out.

I don't know what Ross thought about while he was in his.

It took weeks, but eventually we made peace with the spaces separation had left in our lives and worked to find our way back to each other. We made peace on our first official couch, purchased with money I'd squirreled away during deployment, we made peace in the kitchen with loud music and dinners of real food in portions enough for two, we made peace in the garage and started unpacking the wall of boxes, and we made peace in the bedroom, where I eventually forgot about my towel again.

CHAPTER 13

When Ross and I were first dating, we took a trip to climb the Flatirons in Boulder, Colorado. I had never climbed real cliffs before, only the brightly colored plastic knobs of indoor climbing gyms. You feel realistically human-sized in a climbing gym, substantial and weighty, and people on the floor are able to hear you when you say you are terrified and they offer suggestions about where you might want to put your foot next, or they just say reassuringly, "You're not going to die." On a real cliff face, you are an afterthought, lint, something that may or may not blow away with the next strong wind. Your voice feels tiny, a squeak under the great blue dome of indifferent sky, and there is no guarantee that anyone can hear it.

At one particularly bad moment, I was clinging with two fingers and a toe to a wall with no other visible holds, and Ross was so far above me, and the wind was so strong, that he never heard me shouting, and then all-out screaming, for him to let some slack into the rope so I could remaneuver. I couldn't see what was above or below me, but I knew there was a very real chance I would finally find out if our knots were well tied. I cried and leaned my face into the cold, iron-tasting rock, waiting to see if I would lose bladder control or my shaking fingers and toe would give out or the next strong wind would shove me off my hold. None of that happened. Instead I took a deep, shaky breath and somehow found another toehold.

Ross would have anchored me if I had fallen. He would have felt a sudden tug and I would have felt the springiness and give built into the rope as I dangled like a spider, swinging back and forth in front of the rock, trying not to choke on my own thundering heart. But I didn't fall. Maybe I was too afraid to fall. I trusted him then, but I trust him even more now, having come closer, metaphorically, to falling in the years since when he was even farther away with the rope. But I've still never actually fallen, and the possibility is magnetic and cold at the back of my mind.

Trust does not, however, protect us from the gap in our experiences with climbing. I was inexperienced, afraid, and out of my element; he was not. I was screaming for slack into a wind that swallowed my voice and he was leaning comfortably against a high ledge chatting with our climbing partners, a freakishly talented rescue climber named Russell (whose thumbs stuck out at perfect right angles from his wrists and who had just demonstrated the night before that he could climb the unadorned brick wall of a pub to its roof) and his equally at-home-with-heights girlfriend, Kat. When I finally scrabbled my way onto their ledge, the switch from pure fear coursing through my veins to molten rage was quick.

"Could you not hear me screaming at you for slack?" I tried

to ask this slowly, evenly, through gritted teeth, but I think it came out more as a strangled screech.

"What? Oh! No. I couldn't, sorry! Ready for the next pitch?"

"No, I'm not. I'm going back down, and you can finish. I'm done. I'll wait for you at the bottom."

Halfway up an eight-hundred-foot cliff face, on a tiny lip of rock only feet away from another couple, to whom you are literally tied with many complicated knots, is not a convenient place to try to have your first fight. The reality of the situation, which Ross patiently explained, was that I could not go back down, not without everyone else going back down, and that the climb down was actually longer and more difficult than the climb up, and given what time it was, we could either continue on and rappel down the short back side of the rock as planned, or try to complete the complicated downward climb in darkness. Another thing learned: just because there is no other option but to continue on your present course does not mean you continue on happily. At least, not at first.

The counterweight to all of this was the dizzy, stupid-happy, chest-thumping pride of being able to stand on the jagged ridge at the top of the rock face and stare down at the evening unfolding over Boulder, on one side, and the empty blackness of the rock's hollowed-out back on the other. It took us all day to finish the climb, but there was a sharpness to the feeling of completing it, an aloneness that was not isolating but exhilarating. *Not everyone can do this thing we just did.* Better than that, though—being out on that high, sharp edge in the dark with someone who loved me, and who said, quietly and completely without irony, "I knew you could do this."

We rappelled down off the back of the cliff in total darkness, an absolute act of faith. I leaned back, surrendering my center of gravity, and lowered myself gradually into a muffling nothingness, completely unaware of where the ground was until I bumped gently into it. Going up, he went first, setting the rope; going down, it was me first, finding my feet and then preparing to lower him into the black with me. I looked up from the darkness and focused on Ross, on the stars coming out around him, on the edge of the cliff we'd just climbed. A totally unexpected feeling of peace wrapped itself around me and I let the rope slide through my hands, gently controlling the descent. The rope connected us, we trusted it, and neither of us could see what was next.

I remember climbing the Flatirons when I think about how the first deployment tested us. I remember rappelling into the dark side of the cliff when I think about how we decided to have a baby. Five months after he got back, we finally agreed that there would never be a "right" time, and that there would always be long stretches where I would be solo parenting. On the horizon for his squadron was another, longer deployment the following winter to Afghanistan, and we knew that meant another cycle of month-long work-ups in advance of the actual leaving. I still had another semester in graduate school. But that winter we had a window.

We planned a trip to hike through the Redwoods and snowshoe around Crater Lake, and while we camped in the rain and stayed in a series of tiny cabins packed deep in the snow, I checked my temperature and drew little asterisks on the calendar, adding the ebb and flow of my ovulations to many other colored lines I was keeping track of. We collected visitor center stamps in a small blue National Parks Passport and talked about where we wanted to take our kids camping when they were old enough. I dreamed of names, and nicknames for those names. Ross planned monthly contributions to college accounts. Neither of us mentioned Afghanistan.

I wanted it to be there, on that postdeployment winter vacation at Crater Lake, among the snowy trees and cobalt blue of a water-filled volcano, that we conceived a new life, miles from the Navy and with Ross's "freedom beard" in full bloom, but the universe evidently has a sense of humor and persistent way of making its point about how much control you have just because you can read a calendar. For all my careful color-coding of our schedules—my school, work, and ovulations laid over his work and frequent absences—and the pitiably few number of times it all matched up, our son went from being an idea to a reality on a weekend when it was never supposed to happen. It was two months after our vacation, and I had tagged along with Stella and her kids for another six-hour drive down the California coast to San Diego, where the squadron was on a training detachment. According to what I thought was a pretty solid pattern in my ovulation and inconclusive evidence from the thermometer, I had already ovulated and missed the window. Ross and I had less than thirty-six hours together. Stella, who had logged more hours listening to me work through my longing to be a mother than anyone else, grinned at me on the drive home and asked, "So—feeling pregnant?"

"Ha. Unlikely."

But for the first time in five months, the egg had been late.

The first law of calendars, that they chart and track time in predictable ways, was broken. That was January 2010. The baby was due in October. The squadron was scheduled to leave in early January 2011. With no idea how it would all turn out, we checked our ropes and leaned back into the blackness.

CHAPTER 14

The second law of calendars is that their smaller measured units—days, weeks, months—all add up to the same amount of time for each year, give or take a day or so, adding up to a complete orbit around the sun. We broke this law in 2010, a year that came and went somehow in a far shorter interval than the 365 days it promised. During this truncated time, our first son was born and we made it from one end of the year to the other—without a deployment—seeing each other in short bursts for a combined total of seven weeks. I am tempted to include a chart, but even that would miss some essential truth about what it was like, how it all happened. Ross and I actually had to sit down with our day planners and plow through old e-mails to try to piece it together. Some of the absences were planned, some were surprises, some were the result of error, and some were billed as "opportunities." Nearly all involved acronyms.

Take a deep breath. Here we go: January was for "TAC D&E bullshit" at Naval Air Station North Island in San Diego, where nearly everything broke and a jet got struck by lightning (no one was hurt, but the electrical system got fried). One weekend, I showed up for thirty-six hours and Ross got me pregnant.

In February, he went to the East Coast for LSO School to get certified as a landing signals officer. This was the "opportunity" for a new credential. Hurray!

In March, the squadron went to Fallon, Nevada, for SFARP, which marked the start of work-ups for the next scheduled deployment to Afghanistan the following January. Whatever the hell SFARP means has been explained to me multiple times and I still can't remember. Somewhere in here I stopped throwing up into a Big Gulp cup in my car on the way to work and grad school in the mornings because my first trimester was over.

April meant three weeks on an aircraft carrier off the coast of San Diego with no phone contact for TSTA, another mystery acronym, and it was during TSTA that the *Deepwater Horizon* caught fire and sank in the Gulf of Mexico and I became addicted to Googling satellite images of the spreading spill and wallowing in a deep sense of foreboding.

At some point in early May, Ross was able to drop back in long enough to see our bean-shaped boy on an ultrasound and get all teary-eyed with me, and then in one particularly mystifying week, my parents flew out to California to see Fresno State declare me one of its top graduate students and then lay me off from my job working for the program that awarded me my degree. So much for worrying about maternity leave! During this same week, I became convinced that my father was going to have a heart attack because he spent most of his visit holed up in Ross's study checking and rechecking his e-mail, refusing to eat, and occasionally hollering out profanities at people whose names I didn't recognize along with updates on the worsening crisis on the Gulf Coast. I was furious at him and sad for him at the same time, and when President Obama finally called a moratorium on all off-shore drilling and Dad's project in the Arctic got put on hold, my mom and I returned to the house one day to find him throwing a tennis ball for my dog and looking like he'd won something. Which I guess he had: time. But the next day it was time for everybody to leave again because it was—

June, and time for nine weeks on a boat off the coast of Hawaii in a joint training exercise called RIMPAC, but which everybody called RIMJOB because it was an unplanned absence that got penciled in. During this time I cleaned out my desk at work and found that my world shrank drastically as my belly expanded. At home, swelling and swatting flies in the oppressive Central Valley heat, I plunged myself headlong into a research spiral on unmedicated birth, breastfeeding, sleep training, and social science theories on infant development. I became an ardent fan of "studies" that "suggested," and took worrying to dizzying new heights.

Ross came back from RIMPAC in the first week of August to gasp at my size and lay his ear against the tumult in my belly and attend a quick baby shower at Stella's house before packing up again two weeks later for Air Wing Fallon, a month-long pretend war waged over the Nevada desert. We started talking about baby names via text message.

He came back in mid-September, and would have had to leave again before our son was born had someone not managed to break an aircraft carrier in San Diego, causing the detachment for COMPTUEX/JTFEX (composite training unit exercise/joint task force exercise) to "slide to the right." But slide it did, and

I was just able to toss out some basic instructions to Ross about how he was to step in now and be my birth coach (the books I had been reading suggested that we should have prepared for this months in advance with joint breathing exercises and extensive visualization, but oh, well). We muddled our way through with last-minute emergency repairs to the Honda, more dog X-rays, and a base-wide power outage all converging on our son's birth day, and then two weeks later, with my mom arriving just in time as backup, Ross left again for another month and didn't return until late November, when we were finally able to enjoy the bulk of our time together that year.

Keep in mind that this was all leading up to a combat deployment in January, one that was slated to last anywhere from seven to nine months. Ross was scheduled to have "rolled out" of the squadron only a few months into the deployment, meaning he'd have finished his time with them and moved on to his next job, which is called a "shore tour," but since they were going to Afghanistan and he was by then a senior pilot, the plan was to extend his tour and keep him through the whole deployment. This would have meant missing most of our son's first year. Many people in the military have a story like this. Many have much worse ones.

However, a couple of months earlier, Ross had applied to TOPGUN, hoping to be accepted to the famed tactics course at Naval Air Station Fallon in Nevada and then, once he completed it, to serve out his shore tour for the next three years as a TOPGUN instructor. If he was accepted, the skipper would allow him to roll out on time. As long shots go, it was such a big one that neither of us allowed ourselves to think of it as a genuine possibility, so when it actually did come through, the sensation I remember most was not one of elation or celebration but rather stunned, almost disbelieving relief.

And that was 2010.

Trying to plot our movements for those twelve months, I imagine Ross existing in a cold, dry airborne world, where the oxygen is thin and all voices are tinny and sharp and carry information in precise, carefully timed bursts. I imagine the weeks flying by but also dragging somehow, like the disparity between what your airspeed feels like compared to your relative ground speed. I imagine the scratchiness of the sheets in the variety of temporary beds he slept in and I wonder if he ever had any of those night wakings where you have to wonder for long moments where you are or what day it is.

For me, pregnancy was a waterlogged and murky state. The simultaneous endings of graduate school and my job plunged me into a dense swamp of stunned inaction. My memory dulled, my emotions saturated and overflowed, and my dreams rose up around my ankles, their imagery and messages suddenly vibrant, crystal clear, and invasive. The need for sleep threatened to overtake every other imperative. Bloated, elusive, moody, and strange, I became a sea creature. From July on, I tried to spend as much time in swimming pools as possible. I carried in my mind a map of all available public restrooms ranked by cleanliness as well as a rotating roster of pools, both public and private, in which I could swim laps or just float. This was not a miserable time. Quite the opposite. While I didn't feel like I emitted any kind of glow, I did feel like I was engaged in some kind of constant secret conversation with my body and the tumbling presence inside. I was never alone.

One night stands out in particular. I lumbered from our little white-walled house on Hellcat Court to the small pool at the new community center on base, which Ross and I joked was the community center that was built right by the other community center because we needed more centers for community. The pool was only four feet deep and maybe ten meters long, but having the entire thing to myself, at night, in silence, more than made up for its size. I swam a little, short laps back and forth that shook the underwater lamplight and sent zigzags of bluish gold slicing across the tiles and licking up the concrete walls of the cabana. The water tasted a little salty, and crepe myrtle blossoms floated like flattened fandango skirts on the surface among drowning bugs.

Eventually I stopped in the middle of the pool, put my kickboard behind my head, and floated on my back. I never floated well until I was pregnant. I usually have to keep my arms and legs spinning in a slow gallop to stay afloat. With each deep breath in, I floated higher until my belly, with our still-unnamed boy's knees tucked just underneath, broke the surface; and then as I exhaled, he submerged again. I looked up and saw satellites. I think they were satellites. I couldn't tell if they were moving or if it was my own slow drift. The light from the pool below me washed out the dimmer stars, but the ones I watched seemed to flash red and blue in alternation. I know some stars do this, but I preferred to think that what I was looking at could look back, that far away some automatic camera was recording a tiny, lighted blue postage stamp with a dark kicking speck in it—me, bug sized, among the other bugs. In between me and the satellites, I noticed jets coming and going, formation flights, and I made note of how each wingman was lining up. Between me and the jets, closest and hardest to see, were little brown bats darting around and zipping bugs out of the air, bugs drawn by the refractory light and the smell of the pool.

If I were a poet, I would write my son a poem about this moment, this long series of moments, where I lay on my back and felt him moving slowly inside me and I took note of satellites, jets, bats, and bugs, things flying and things submerged, when I felt perfectly at peace and in balance, when I could have broken down crying at the richness of everything I was feeling, the luck and beauty of it all. I would end by thanking him over and over again for how he magnified the world for me and made me feel less alone in it, how I would miss him when he wasn't living within my body anymore. Even without a proper name, he had changed the meaning of everything I knew.

A crib, a bassinet, a giant pile of blankets, a breast pump, a feeding pillow, baby carriers, maternity clothes, a shelf-full of books, and a patient accumulation of advice based on experience— these are the gifts Stella and Jake passed on to us as Ross flew and I floated through our year with no time. And while it's true that Ross and I were apart for much of my pregnancy, it's also true that I found myself initiated into a tribe of women, military mothers, who rose up to fill that gap. Advice and hand-me-downs and diapers galore came from everywhere, often uncannily timed so that as soon as I realized I needed something and began to worry, or had begun to formulate a question, the item or bit of advice showed up unbidden with a quiet knock at the door of my house.

Something I'd always suspected was proving to be true: that not having children was like standing in some kind of glass-walled anteroom to the world of military wives, credentialed but not yet fully endorsed. Was it just that we were all so wildly different—different home states, different religions, different educations, different jobs, different pasts—that made child-rearing our one resounding commonality? Partially, I think the answer to that one is yes, but I also think it's more complicated than that. The uncertainty of detachments, of finding yourself suddenly alone in a town far from home or, God forbid, in the midst of a deployment or yet another relocation—the act of bringing a baby into this particular world seems like even more of a high-wire act than it might otherwise be. We know, in a heightened sense, how much we need each other despite our differences, and how much more complicated the road ahead is about to get.

And no matter who you are, or who you were before, the weird, murky months of growing from one person into two makes you see the world with different eyes. Threats pop up that didn't seem like threats only the day before, and the world suddenly becomes aware of the plural you and your changed physical space in a way it wasn't before. Oddly enough, beyond the immediate concerns of managing his birth, the road ahead didn't worry me as much as the one behind. Our boy would get out into the world somehow, and he would get a name once he got there. What was more troubling was how the past, the brush with the idea of splitting up in Singapore and our hesitant and bumpy reunion after the deployment, brought to mind other failures. My disastrous teenage years kept surfacing in my dreams. Failure, being shamed and ostracized, losing my grip on the world, and being wholly without community—the dark days of the dawn of my depression—all of these came bubbling up in the months of my pregnancy to speak to me again.

CHAPTER 15

My parents had a terrific fight the night before dropping me off at boarding school. It was our first trip together outside of Saudi Arabia, and we'd just spent two weeks driving around the Scottish Highlands so my parents could replay the highlights of their early marriage and the beginnings of our family for Doug and me. It was a beautiful trip, but most of our pictures show me scowling in ripped jeans and a Nirvana T-shirt. I knew they'd all be going back to Saudi Arabia without me, and as much as I'd been confused and unnerved by my time there, it felt even weirder to be separating from my family.

I'd chosen St. Stephen's Episcopal School in Austin, Texas, because I wanted to be near something familiar, even though the school itself was tucked way out in the swanky northwestern hills. Everything had been squared away for months—after our brief vacation, we would come back to Texas, camp out for a few days in the house in Georgetown, now empty since the renters had moved out, drop me and a trunkful of clothes off at boarding school, and then my parents and Doug would head back to Saudi. But at the last minute, my mother balked, simply digging in her heels and saying, "No. I can't do it. This is wrong."

My dad countered with all the logical arguments—the long-term plan, prior measured discussions, reassurances about my maturity and the quality of the school—but she wouldn't budge and they both got loud. Ultimately, my dad asked me to make the final call. Honestly, it pissed me off. I was nervous about going to boarding school, but for the last year I'd been told this was the only option. I was fifteen years old, my bags were packed, and I already had a checkbook and a checking account in my name. My family was depending on me. Of course I went.

I was assigned to room 20 in "New Dorm," so named even though it was more than four years old. A holdup in the paperwork to dedicate our building to a wealthy donor lasted until after another, newer dorm was built, named Towner House, and populated with other multiaddress girls. My room on the second floor had gray linoleum floors, two recessed closets with no doors on them, two black metal frame twin beds with four-inch-thick mattresses, and two battered wooden desks, mine with the word "FUCK" carved deeply into its surface. The room's right side had already been claimed by my roommate, a tennis prodigy named Melanie from a town near Dallas.

My parents walked me around to find the coin-operated laundry room and the hall pay phone. This was in the days before cell phones, voice mail, and e-mail. This pay phone, shared with twenty other girls who may or may not pass on any messages they received, was my lifeline. A fax machine tucked away in the administrative office was the only way to exchange documents for signatures or get written permission to leave campus. And then, of course, there was international mail.

Having no parents in the country and no driver's license made me a custody problem when holidays rolled around, and meant foisting me off on various relatives. I never felt unwelcome wherever I went, and I always enjoyed myself (if not quite behaved myself—I got drunk for the first time with my cousin over Thanksgiving break in Lubbock). But the getting-there part, the logistics headache, made me remember the times in junior high when my newly laid-off dad was supposed to pick me up from after-school band practice and forgot, and all my teachers, and then the principal, and then the janitors each checked their watches and offered me rides, which I turned down on the conviction that my dad was *just now* on his way. It happened so many times that even now I will gladly pay exorbitant cab fees rather than rely on a friend for a ride home from anywhere.

When it came time to travel, I lied to my parents and said someone from boarding school was giving me a ride; I lied to the school and said relatives were. In reality, I went to great lengths to schedule my driver's ed hours to coincide with times I needed to get to the airport, and to save enough holiday money for a cab back to school. The only one to ever question my plan was my driver's ed instructor, an ex-cop named Rodney who had a torso like an overstuffed couch cushion and little, underused legs. When he found out I was flying back and forth to Saudi Arabia by myself over Christmas break, he stared at my profile for a long time while the driving school's Saturn struggled up the steep hills of the isolated road leading away from St. Stephen's and then said, "I'd never let my kid do that."

It was complicated, how I felt when he said that, and I struggled to keep my mind on the road. Bafflement was the first emotion to pop up, with the thought, *Why not? Airports are some of the easiest places in the world—there are signs everywhere,* and then defensiveness, *You don't know my family and you don't know me,* and then, finally, deep sadness.

It was beginning to happen to me around this time, the long, dark fogs that wouldn't lift, the depression passed down from my dad. I didn't yet have a name for it or understand how deep it would eventually get or how isolating. All I knew at the time was that the day's accumulated tasks—getting up and going to mandatory chapel before classes, eating cafeteria food, checking my mailbox, going to soccer practice, watching the school's majority day student population get picked up at the end of the day, and then attending mandatory study hall in the library with a mountain of homework for the evening—just felt absolutely pointless.

At St. Stephen's, I became a soloist in several senses. There had been a school band in Saudi Arabia, and I had played in it, but the band's skill level was so abysmal that when we played the warm-up note on the first day of school, hot tears sprang to my eyes and I stopped my breath and let the note die in my mouth.

St. Stephen's had no band or orchestra at the time, so I was offered private lessons with a university professor. I learned solo pieces to a piano accompaniment, but the pianist could only make it out to our campus in the hills once or twice a month. I was supposed to imagine her line, an abbreviated version of which was sketched out in tiny ghost script over my own so I would know how long to rest and when to come back in. I tried for a couple of weeks to learn the music by practicing in my dorm room, but one day a girl stuck her head in and said that she hated the sound of the clarinet, that it put her nerves on edge. From then on, I practiced by assembling only the middle two joints of the horn, making a headless and footless version of my instrument and practicing just the fingering. I figured I was already imagining one voice in the piece, so why not make it two? Thus in silence I learned part of a Weber clarinet concerto, which, when I finally performed it for a morning chapel assembly, showed amply the pitfalls of silent, solo, and sporadic practice.

I had friends during this period, or at least I assume I did because people were always hanging out in my dorm room. I had boyfriends. I played on the soccer team and made good grades except for Spanish. I eventually earned a driver's license by taking weekend driving classes. All verifiable facts, but the truth is that I wasn't there at all. Initially, I'd bonded intensely with my roommate, Melanie, but then she was gone most of the time for tennis tournaments and practices. I had a friend from Saudi who lived down the hall from me, Erin, but she was a legit, lifelong Aramco brat who had grown up with the expectation of leaving home at fifteen for boarding school. None of this, I gathered, seemed the slightest bit weird or lonely to her—on the contrary, she seemed excited and invigorated by her newfound freedom. I tuned out nearly everyone but Lauren, a moody girl with whom I shared a physical resemblance striking enough for us to be continually mistaken for each other. Her pissed-off, anti–boarding school rants found a receptive audience in me, and we hunkered down together in our anger at this place where we were both trapped.

I had a faculty mentor, Miss Healy, who was some sort of social coordinator, and at whose small apartment I was required, with a few other boarder girls, to check in every morning before chapel. She was an ardent Disney fan with a round face, short blond curls, and a bubbly personality, and she made it abundantly clear from the first time we met that she didn't like me. The one time I visited her outside of our required morning meetings to talk about my feelings of depression, she took multiple long calls over the course of our conversation, giving me the "just a minute" finger but seeming in no hurry to wrap up her conversations, until I finally excused myself, embarrassed.

So while these things were true, it was also true that along with maintaining only the bare minimum of contact with my family, enough to prove I was alive and to continue getting a small allowance, I stopped eating much other than Ramen noodles, Doritos, and Dr Pepper from vending machines. I started sneaking out of the dorm at night to cross the dewy soccer fields and wander around in the woods beyond, sometimes with Lauren, who introduced me to weed with a tiny pinch of it that we smoked through holes punched in the dented side of a Dr Pepper can, and sometimes alone, walking for miles hoping to get lost or fall in a hole or off a cliff somewhere.

Months went by in a kind of slow, downhill slide. Christmas came and went with my solo flights to and from Saudi Arabia, a trip during which I'd bailed out on a hesitant conversation with my mom about not wanting to go back to school. Instead, I'd learned that international airlines don't card for booze, and that I could pass the time on an eight-hour flight to Amsterdam by shamelessly making out with some other random sad boy on his way back to a boarding school on the East Coast. When I came back, Lauren broke the news to me that she'd convinced her parents to withdraw her from St. Stephen's and bring her back home.

She promised to write, and in her one letter was a suggestion that maybe over spring break she could come get me. "Can you say ROAD TRIP??"

A new element added to my solo night walks, one that seemed to arise out of nowhere. I discovered that if I used my Swiss Army knife, the one my dad bought me in a shop in al-Khobar, to slowly carve intersecting lines into my forearms and shins, I could achieve a temporary high, the singular feeling that for once I knew exactly where I was on the globe.

It shouldn't have been much of a surprise that I got expelled from boarding school, but nevertheless, I was surprised when it happened. Mr. Bell summoned me from American history class to ask me about a particular night more than a month prior in which Lauren and I, with Melanie home early from a tournament and joining us at the last minute, had dropped acid in the dorm. None of us had any prior experience with psychedelics, and we had in fact not even intended to buy acid. Lauren and I had handed eighty dollars in cash to a senior girl in another dorm and, in total ignorance about prices or quantities, just asked for "as much pot as that will buy, or hash if you can find it." Presented the next day with five hits of acid and no instructions on how to take it beyond "Have fun!" we'd each taken one hit, and then, convinced the drug wasn't doing anything, I'd taken the other two. Lauren and Melanie did okay, from what I can remember, but my trip took a different direction and I ended up spending the next twelve hours pacing the halls and grinding my teeth until eventually a nice girl who lived on the first floor realized what was going on and let me into her room. She'd had a bad trip before too, and she sat talking soothing nonsense to me, mother-to-baby words, until I came back down, sometime in the gray early morning hours.

The drug itself, and then the two-week mega-flu that followed, seemed like punishment enough, so Mr. Bell's sudden, grave curiosity about the event felt redundant and also sort of improbable, since he could have named almost any weekend in the past six months and found some sort of major infraction to ask questions about.

At any rate, there was a reckoning to be had with Mr. Bell and it was overdue. Our first encounter yielded nothing. I denied everything and went back to class and then on to soccer practice, which was apparently sufficient time for him to question Melanie, call her parents, and have them drive down and withdraw her from school, leaving behind only a few clanking hangers and a scrawled Post-it Note from her that read, "I told them everything. I'm sorry. I'll miss you." The next two days were a blur. I recall one other meeting, perhaps during classes, in which I continued my attempt to stonewall, but by now other students were nervously pulling me aside and making threats. "You'd better not let my name drop. I can find you wherever you end up."

What I remember is the third meeting. It was late evening and about to rain and they took me to an administrative building I'd never been inside. The hall outside Mr. Bell's office had plants and low lighting, but the office itself was small, bright, and covered in piles of paper. Empty soft drink cups crowded the ledges of the bookcase and a white plastic clock high on the wall to my left drew my eyes like a magnet. Three adults took turns in the room with me: Mr. Bell, who was the assistant headmaster (I never met the actual one); Ms. McCallum, who was my soccer coach but also had some other official title; and Mr. Calvin, to whom I'd submitted a drawing for the school's literary magazine, but whose purpose in a disciplinary sense was otherwise unclear to me.

Mr. Bell's red tie was loosened and his sleeves rolled back over crossed arms. He regarded me from behind his mountain of papers with bloodshot eyes and laid out a pretty accurate account of the night in question, up to and including my stay in the infirmary.

"So the three of you took the drugs, you got sick, Lauren left, we found out about all of it and got the truth from Melanie. Is that about the long and short of it?" I figured this admission was safe—Lauren and Melanie were already gone and Mr. Bell was clearly determined to finish up the job by kicking me out. This seemed fair. "Yes."

"Good," he said. "So now all we need to know is where you got the drugs." Here again, I spoke what I considered, then and now, to be truth, and accidentally lit myself on fire in the process.

"There are lots of drugs here," I said. "Getting them was easy. It took one afternoon. That's all I'm going to say." I truly felt that this was a fair answer, but maybe it wasn't. I had no interest in protecting the identity of the girl who'd bought us the acid. Neither did I care about protecting the names of the friends who had either stopped talking to me or started openly threatening me. I guess I just felt like offering up my head on the chopping block was a fair exchange for admission of guilt, and that anything more should require a little more work on his part. I offered one other detail, the part about taking the extra hits and having a bad trip, thinking, stupidly, that he might view it as I had, as a possible down payment on punishment. This seemed to irritate Mr. Bell and he walked out of the room. I started crying at this point and continued on and off throughout the rest of my time in his office, gradually working my way through an entire box of tissues.

Ms. McCallum seemed a little more sympathetic. She had

seen some promise in me during soccer season and had asked me to start practicing with the varsity squad. She had a way of doing a bear claw motion and braying, "Awwwww, sick 'em, Bears!" for her alma mater that was both self-deprecating and obviously deeply proud. We talked about my parents, about school. I tried to explain my position to her, but she insisted that for things to get better for everyone, I had to give them somewhere to start. I think my silence disappointed us both.

Mr. Calvin seemed uncomfortable with the whole tag-team arrangement. He looked miserable and spent a long moment bent over in his chair with his head in his hands. I waited for him to say something, and when he didn't, I said, "I've told Mr. Bell what I did that night. I'm not saying I didn't do anything wrong. I don't remember the whole chain of events exactly after we took the drugs, but . . ."

"On multiple hits of acid? Who would?" His laugh was short and bitter, a sharp puff of air from the nostrils. He was quiet again for a long time and then he said something that completely surprised me. "Look, whatever happens from here, there's more to life than this, okay? It gets better." Then we just sat quietly in the room together, him watching the clock and me killing off tissues and staring at the floor.

Ms. McCallum came back and asked about depression. Or maybe she asked how I was doing with being homesick. Or maybe she just talked about soccer again. Whatever it was, maybe even without meaning to, she moved some of the electricity out of the air. She created room for possibility. Maybe Ms. McCallum would understand about my arms, and why I always kept the city map of long, puckering cuts hidden beneath long sleeves. I didn't mean to gross her out or upset her, but when I rolled up my sleeves she said, "Hold on. I'm going to step out for a moment and I'll be *right back*." I was rebuttoning my cuffs when she came back in and brought up Charter Lane Hospital.

"It's a safe place. They can look after you for a while."

Maybe no one meant for this to sound like a threat, like the consequence for not giving up names was a trip to the mental hospital whose commercials Doug and I had grown up watching on TV and frequently imitated ("I don't *need* your help," "I can quit anytime!," "Don't worry—I'll cut down," with the ominous echo, "down, down, down"). Maybe the intent really was to act "in loco parentis" and to prevent future damage.

Mr. Bell's final offer came after a long hiatus in the interrogation, during which I studied the chaos of his office and concluded that he was definitely a dick, but was probably also overworked. He spelled it out in between heavy pauses and grinds of his jaw: the possibility to reenroll after a "break," during which he would recommend that I get in-patient treatment for my "emotional problems," *if* I gave names. It would not have to be an expulsion. He indicated that my parents had not yet been notified, and it seemed like he felt this was a bargaining chip that gave him leverage. I could tell he was angry. I could tell what he thought of me. What I couldn't tell was what he would do if I continued trying to deal with this by myself. I told him I needed the night to think and he finally let me go.

Even though it was long past lights out, and evidently something she'd been advised against doing, my dorm mother, a woman I barely knew, let me use the hall pay phone to place one call. "Witch hazel," she said. "Witch hazel for those eyes." Years later when I heard she had died of cancer the sudden crush of sadness surprised me.

The connection to Saudi Arabia fuzzed, clicked, and fumbled, and when my dad picked up the phone I could tell he'd been sleeping. It was early morning there. "Dad, I'm getting kicked out of school for drugs."

"Well."

The silence that followed was so long that I wondered if he was still there. "Dad?" My ability to imagine other possibilities faltered here. Had my dad not said what he said next, I don't know what I would have done.

"We still love you." And then, "We're coming to get you."

My uncle Dan, a first mate in the merchant marine, arrived back in town from his latest stint on a ship just in time to get a call from my parents asking him to go and pick me up from St. Stephen's while they scrambled to arrange emergency travel visas back to the United States. For all of the angst I've felt about the disappearing men in my life, Dan's arrival in the wake of my boarding school disaster was nothing short of a miracle. He was the uncle I knew best, and his showing up at the front door off and on throughout my childhood, most often in the bleak stretches when my dad was away, always felt like some unexpected treat. And now here he was, only two miserable days after my encounter with Mr. Bell, helping me toss the contents of my dorm room into crumbling produce boxes I'd stolen from behind the school kitchen and then load them into the back of his pickup truck. He looked shocked at first, and allowed me to remain completely silent for the first half hour of our trip back up I-35 to the empty house in Georgetown, but then he cranked up the volume on R.E.M.'s "Shiny Happy People," gave me a fully ironic grin, and asked if I wanted tacos before we hit up the storage unit for a few essentials.

A slow backtracking movement began after my expulsion from boarding school. After liberating my bed, the TV, some boxes of dishes and towels, and a futon mattress he set up for himself in the study, Dan took on the job of babysitting me long-term, which somehow ended up not feeling awkward for me at all. We ate lots of fast food and watched *The Simpsons* and *My So-Called Life* together every night. He let me talk, or not talk, as I chose, and kept reassuring me that I was not the biggest failure he knew, despite the fact that Miss Healy, perhaps anticipating her own shit storm in the wake of my expulsion, had taken a parting shot before I left school and suggested to me coldly that perhaps, if my parents managed to stay together through all of this, I might eventually be able to complete my GED. Each morning I would wake up and have a few seconds of peace before the reality of the empty house sifted down over me, and what it meant, what I'd done to end up there.

My parents flew in from Saudi Arabia five days after I'd been rescued from St. Stephen's, or after I'd slunk away with my tail between my legs with a pickup load of bad memories—I saw it both ways. Dan and I met them at baggage claim at Robert Mueller Municipal Airport, where it quickly became evident that they harbored a similar contradictory view of my situation. They handed me a bundle of fresh flowers wrapped in plastic, stared at me with a tender kind of horror, said that they loved me, and then slowly warmed up to berating me the whole way back to Georgetown.

Meetings with the school administrators took place over the next few days; my parents took a yellow legal pad, whether to actually take notes in order to study the problem on paper or to appear serious, grim, and potentially litigious, I don't know. They had a lot to sort out. Neither side would have been telling them the whole truth, that I know for sure. I wasn't about to lay it all out there, since I was still unsure of where I would be shuffled off to next or how my transgressions registered on the scale of Bad, Bad Shit according to my parents. I also have trouble believing the school officials painted an accurate portrait of their lackluster engagement with the small boarding population, or the fact that it would have taken an already thriving drug culture among the student population, day students and boarders alike, to ramp me up from sneaking the occasional cigarette in Saudi Arabia to smoking pot, boozing on airplanes, and dropping acid in the space of a few short months.

I did a lot of snarling and pouting during this period, a lot of lying on my back and listening to Nine Inch Nails albums on repeat and writing overwrought journal entries, and much of this was in reaction to the bitter irony that though it was ostensibly my drug use that had gotten me into this mess, I was now being told I needed more drugs to get me out. Another stop on the meeting circuit was with a series of psychiatrists, notably omitting the one the school recommended, who had already set his little tape recorder in front of me a few days after the interrogations, but before my uncle came to get me, and asked what about my childhood at home had made me turn to drugs. Finally, a handsome, white-haired neuropsychiatrist with an expansive Texas drawl was chosen to treat me for what was termed "major depression." I took a page from my parents' playbook and brought a yellow legal pad to the first few appointments and wrote my own sullen observations of him, which he gamely allowed.

Wellbutrin, Zoloft, Paxil, and finally Prozac were called up in turn to marshal my faulty neurotransmitters, all in wrenching tweaks of dosage that left me with nightmares, mood swings, bouts of full-body itchiness, and nervous tooth grinding that made my jaw and temples sore. The worst part was not being able to spot my own side effects first. I hated having to rely on other people's impressions of me, or to have one of my seemingly logical rants on the trap of being female, the drudgery and enslavement of careers, or the general pointlessness of life met with a cocked head and bemused gaze and the observation, "This dosage seems maybe a little high."

Within a couple of months of my parents' mop-up emergency visit, my mother was back for good, hauling my brother in tow, who had been given just enough time to finish ninth grade back in Saudi Arabia before having it broken to him that he would not be headed off to boarding school himself. Doug had had a great ninth grade year in Saudi, had in fact blossomed into a social butterfly and was looking forward to the chance to play competitive private school soccer, but he took the change of plans in stride. The furniture was back. Our dog, cared for by family while we were gone and now enormously fat from table scraps, was back. We had family dinners again and there were lights on in other rooms of the house while I lay in mine, trying to figure out what it meant, or if it would all stay. My mother watched me and fed me and frowned at me and made me keep my bedroom door open. She clacked handfuls of vitamins on my breakfast plate next to the eggs and she dragged me around with her on errands, getting the house back in order. She insisted on conversation.

Predictably, I fought all this mothering. When she threw out the tie-dyed tapestry with Jim Morrison on it that I'd hung over the fluorescent lights in my room at boarding school and that was now hanging over my bed at home, she said, "You don't need this counterculture bullshit. This isn't even your generation." I didn't even listen to the Doors and had inherited the tapestry from someone at school, but I put up a fight anyway. My point was, *Who are you to come in and question my decisions now? You gave that up, remember?*

We fought often, mostly because I'd lost my childhood fear of saying the wrong thing and triggering a blowup. I was looking for it now, and I knew what to say, or when to needle her with my stony silence and flattened stare. When I look back, my sixteen-year-old self insists my mom was throwing up all kinds of arbitrary rules and boundaries, that she was changing the game after being complicit in screwing it up in the first place, but the only law from this period I can remember is "get out of bed and get dressed before ten," the letter of which I obeyed by getting up, dragging on pants, straightening the covers, and lying back down again with my eyes open. She may even have suggested I start thinking about the inevitable task of reenrolling in the tenth grade, but she might as well have asked me to build a functioning jet engine out of Lincoln Logs or redirect the San Gabriel River running through the center of our town. I was so used to feeling ordered around that exercising my own will, pulling myself up by my bootstraps, left me wanting only to dig my heels in and embrace immobility and silence.

One night in particular comes to mind. I don't know what triggered it, but I decided to come sit in the living room on the ledge of our fireplace hearth, facing my mother on the couch where she had been watching TV, and shout the most awful accusations I could think of, accusations that would echo back at me years later when I found myself married to a Navy man and moving all the time. I told her she was too weak to have left my dad when it would have done her any good; that she put up with a completely unreasonable cycle of abandonments and that it had scarred me permanently and look, now I'm crazy; that she had given me up when I was fifteen because she and my dad were too suckered by a stupid paycheck and that if they had been more creative—or stronger, or smarter, or *something*—they could have made it work living back here; that neither of them loved me and I hated them back and that they had taken the one thing in the whole world that made any sense, a family, and broken it. I shouted until I was hoarse. She never moved, except once early on, to point the remote at the TV and turn it off. Her face darkened and she crossed her arms over her stomach and listened, and at the end, she said through gritted teeth something so weird and out of character I knew immediately it had come from my psychiatrist: "I understand that you're upset and I hear you."

And that was it. I didn't feel any better. I felt weird, like I had one night out on the soccer fields at St. Stephen's after the curfew bell when a thunderstorm was blowing in. The air got strange, cottony-feeling, and the hairs on my arms started to rise. I wasn't doing anything that night, or looking for anyone. I was just sitting on the metal bleachers by the field enjoying being in the wrong place, in the dark. When the lightning started it was all at once and in spidery little sideways flashes all around me. The thunder was instantaneous like a punch to the chest, and the air smelled like burned batteries. I was moving before I'd even fully made the decision to go back inside. I felt like I'd walked in on something or accidentally crossed a boundary, and that for all my playacting with small, human-sized risks, this one, being here, was deeply wrong. Shouting those things at my mother felt like that, like I had charged the air and anything could happen. I had called down the specter of a broken family fully ready for it to be true, believing that it already was, but nothing happened. She understood that I was upset and she heard me? What was that? I went back to my room.

After a six-week hiatus from school, which I started calling "the shittiest spring break ever," I enrolled in the last six weeks of tenth grade in what would have been my original public high school. I was just in time for the first chair clarinetist in the b-string band, a girl I'd known in junior high, to get the stomach flu for the year's last concert. I learned her solo, sat in her chair, and tried to reacquaint myself with the sensation of hearing music behind and around me when I played. The bored fluttering of a flutist's fingers on the keys while she waited out a rest, the smell of valve oil and cork grease, the collective in-drawn breath at the start of a piece—I tried to remember and relearn these things as something positive, but the overwhelming sensation was of waking up way past the alarm clock and not knowing where I was.

The next year, I tried to learn to march with the rest of my peers who had already been doing it for two years and managed, barely, not to slam into anyone. The feeling of grogginess, of not being fully awake, pervaded my junior year, and nowhere was the feeling stranger or more acute than when I was standing in the middle of a brightly lit football field with the bells of tubas and trombones flashing in my eyes and an exploding line of snare drums crossing behind my back. We played ridiculous music during marching season—the theme from *Cats* and later something about America—and competed all over the state in our stiff uniforms and snapping formations. The return to music, to having a voice and exercising the will to learn something, and to engage with people in doing it, was painful and strange. It both filled my heart and constricted it. Playing lush orchestral arrangements during concert season was the monsoon joy to the desert freakishness and faux-militarism (which was itself weirdly alluring) of marching season. To this day my most frequent anxiety dreams are of marching out to the middle of a field in long identical lines to the steady tick of a snare drum, not having any clue what music we're about to play or which way I'll have to dodge when the formations start to move.

In the end, I graduated high school as a section leader in the marching band with okay grades and a date to the prom. Partially as penance and partially to prove to myself that I could be cast as a good kid and not some epic screwup, I became an antidrug peer counselor during my senior year and volunteered my time with at-risk elementary school kids.

Yet I wasn't a part of this class any more than I was a part of the wild, globe-trotting crowd from Saudi Arabia or the rich, drugged-out academic elite at St. Stephen's. I show up in two high school yearbooks—St. Stephen's, understandably, deleted me—but I belong in neither. I still have a few friends I keep in touch with from this period, as many as I can count on one hand, but I know I'll never go to any reunions because it will take too much explaining for anyone to remember who I am. I have this crippling fear that even though there are roll sheets and grade records, there won't be a name tag on the table for me to hunt for.

I struggle with this, the degree to which I don't belong in my own past, and the degree to which I passively and then actively rebelled against the direction my story took starting in the summer of 1993. What would it have looked like if I had learned to adapt better, if I had just let things unfold and let down my guard instead of convincing myself that it was all going the wrong direction and that I had to escape?

More to the point, what would it look like if this cycle of periodic aloneness came for me again, if against every intention I somehow re-created it? I liked to think the boarding school debacle taught me something about the value of asking for help, of choosing my confidantes wisely and then trusting them enough to let their strength support me, and offering the same in return. Putting up a front of silent competence ensured that I achieved the exact opposite, but old habits die hard, especially when the initial setup starts to feel familiar. Would there be casualties the next time I found myself alone and in over my head, and if so, would anyone claim me this time after the damage was done?

CHAPTER 16

I was born on a bright, chilly day in early November 1978 in Austin, Texas, neither early nor late nor exactly on time, as there was some general disagreement between my mother and two different doctors about when she could have gotten pregnant according to the calendars and my dad's work schedule. I hadn't even made my debut on the planet and already absences and calendars were exerting their contrary and tidelike influences. Since my actual gestational age was disputed, the fact that I jabbed a hole in my placental home with one finger and started the party on my own timing, was, by all accounts, problematic. My father was not yet home from his shift in the North Atlantic, and when reached by telephone and informed by my mother that she was in labor, his shouted, half-joking advice was, "Stand on your head!"

The delivery doctor, an all-around sleaze who would later impregnate one of his nurses and then perform her abortion as well since he was already married, was not ready for my arrival either. When it became clear that the Pitocin drip would not hurry my arrival by the time his shift ended, he slowed my mother's contractions just enough to extend her labor overnight so he could go home and get some sleep. We spent a long night together, she and I, waiting on the men for whom our introduction had been delayed, for whom our timing was unexpected, inscrutable, a surprise, inconvenient. One man was on his way, hurrying through the fluorescent-lit netherworld of airports and baggage claim and parking garages and taxis. One man was home in bed. Here was my father, bleary eyed and exhausted, collapsing in a chair next to the bed, and a few hours later, here was the doctor, bright eyed and bushy tailed, exclaiming that it was now "time to have this baby!" After an on-and-off Pitocin drip, nearly nineteen hours of inexplicable delays, and a nearly too late epidural, my mother was so exhausted and fed up when I was finally delivered that she waved me off to my father to be bathed, weighed, blinded with eye creams, poked with immunization shots, and introduced to the bright stare of the world.

I offer this story in contrast to my brother's birth in Aberdeen, Scotland, nineteen months later, which was evidently so low-key that my mother spent most of her labor wandering around the shops of downtown Aberdeen before arriving at the hospital (having sent my father home to arrange a babysitter for me), casually losing her mucus plug, or having a "bloody show," neither of which phrase sounds less horrific than the other, and being hustled into a bed to deliver my brother thirty minutes later with no other medical intervention than the brogue-heavy encouragements of a red-faced labor nurse. "The Matty," as the maternity hospital was called, was evidently so overrun with babies that Doug spent days peacefully mucky in his own birth funk and snuggled against my mother's chest while she had tea around a communal table with a bunch of other new mothers and lobbied the doctors for her early release.

As with every story my mother told me, I sucked these in, held on to them, and then puffed them back up into the air like smoke rings to examine their shape and patterns of dissolution. What did they mean, how did they apply to me, and what was I supposed to do differently because they had been given to me? I decided Doug's birth sounded preferable and had possibly shaped his character. He was always more laid-back than me, more adept at enjoying the moment and creating communities of friends on whom he could depend. Maybe this was from sitting at tea listening to Scottish accents in placental funk. I was always the worrier, the overthinker trying so hard to please but bad at extending enough trust to create many strong bonds. Maybe that was from being delivered by an asshole into a room full of exhausted people hastily reunited and watching the clock. Maybe our entrances have weight; very possibly they don't. But after looking so hard and trying to figure it out, I can say this: we try so hard to avoid, correct, edit, and recast the mistakes we think our parents made that, more often than not, we end up slavishly repeating them.

Sam came into the world much as I had—heavily anticipated and wedged into a difficult timeline with a fluctuating and uncertain cast of characters. My pervasive anxiety about his arrival had taken root and flowered into an ornate Birth Plan, a detailed flowchart of premade decisions designed to wring out every last precious ounce of control over the situation I could gain in light of the fact that when the time actually came to have a baby, I would be relying most on the two people I'd seen the least over the course of my pregnancy: Ross and the doctor. I'd seen at least six different doctors and one midwife, the general wisdom among other

Navy wives giving birth at the base hospital being that you should try to meet everyone at least once, since you could end up with anyone.

So when my son started his descent three days early with a mighty contraction that wrenched me awake at the exact moment all the power went off for the scheduled basewide maintenance outage, a day when our dying Honda was in the shop and our dog was scheduled for complicated X-rays, he was, in effect, making a declaration of war against my Plan. It was a war I needed to lose—trying to choreograph every possibility in a birth, especially as a first-timer, is folly—but that didn't make fighting it any less desperate for me. I wanted so much to believe that I had learned something from all the stories I'd absorbed, that I could skip the part where I was scared and fumbling and at the mercy of forces beyond my control and instead plan and research my way into a broad, clear plane of totally expected options.

I fought for this (and failed) especially during the times in which Ross had to leave during my labor—the Honda was the only vehicle we owned capable of carrying an infant car seat, and the dog would need to be boarded, and during these two short and necessary errands that required his presence, I crawled alone up and down the hallway of our hot, dark house, dragging my iPhone with me to time contractions and play a carefully compiled playlist designed to stave off mounting waves of panic. My contractions were two minutes apart, ten minutes apart, four minutes and thirty seconds apart, crushing, mild, and moderate, and my water was leaking noncommittally. In other words, no patterns, no logical progressions. My actions were equally nonsensical: I flipped light switches on and off in every room I entered and made a completely casual phone call to Ross requesting a latte and a pumpkin scone, and then another one, weeping, to my mother, insisting that yes, what I really need right now is to hear, in detail, exactly how her dog's vet appointment went that morning.

Perhaps this much is obvious: things did not go as planned. I scored the Norwegian midwife for my delivery, which felt lucky, until she informed me I had dilated only to five "sontimeters." Meanwhile Ross kept mentioning the ice we had stockpiled in the extra freezer at home in preparation for the scheduled power outage. It might be leaking all over the floor, he said, and he should maybe go and check. I felt my luck start to turn. I knew he hadn't eaten all day and was exhausted. I was using him up, my lifeline; I was crushing him under the weight of my need and we weren't even to the hard part yet—we were barely *halfway*.

When I let out my strident cry of "Uncle!" it was an unpleasant surprise to find that the anesthesiologist was not, in fact, hovering right outside my door rubbing her hands together menacingly with a giant needle clamped in her teeth like a bowie knife. She had to be summoned. Further unexpected delay, coupled with rankling irony: I needed to provide answers to a detailed health questionnaire, including an inventory of all past recreational drug use (the list had grown: I backslid in college). Pink Floyd's "Comfortably Numb" came up on my phone's playlist (of course) and by the time they were ready to place the line and had me sitting upright, naked to the waist and painting my back with iodine, I was unable to keep still and was gyrating like a slow top and burying my face in Ross's chest, moaning and trying quite earnestly to tear a hole in Green Jacket with my teeth. (He wore it, thank God. I will always love him for that.)

Two more monstrous contractions rolled over me before the

epidural took effect. Ross waited with me, holding my hand. I kept my eyes closed, doing a mental pat-down of my body. *Am I all right? Is everything still there? Will I make it through this next part?* I was shuddering violently from the adrenaline, and he asked a nurse if the anesthesia was just local or if it was going to my head. Teeth gritted and only one eye open, I croaked, "What, I don't look fine to you?" He asked me again if it was okay for him to leave, just for a little bit, long enough to run home, if I was sure I'd be all right. I said I was sure I'd be fine, because this gigantic, complete lie seemed like the thing to say.

Why was it so hard for me to imagine a way to say "no" or "please don't leave"? I've thought about this a lot, and the only answer I have is that habit is a strong thing—those words never worked before, and not leaving, for my dad and for Ross, was rarely an option. Plus, I still have this self-conscious horror of making a scene, of letting anyone on the sidelines see me freak out and lose control. Maybe that's the real fear, losing control. Maybe getting left is just the opening salvo for a far sneakier, more personal kind of pain.

I hate to linger here, on the half hour I spent listening to the whir of little machines at my bedside and making small talk with the nurses. It's just that in all my planning, all my imaginings of things going right and things going wrong, I never, ever thought I would have been trumped by an appliance. Still, I was more comfortable than I'd been in hours, days even, and I hadn't been left *alone.* There was something pleasant about having just women around me, strangers, yes, but professionals who looked not at all alarmed about what was happening to my body. This, in contrast to the previous five hours where Ross and I had reflected the same drained panic back at each other as each new position and massage technique failed to alleviate the galloping waves of pain. Even though several years, another birth, and some therapy have allowed me to gain some perspective on what actually went on—that we were both scared and tired and bad at communicating in a critical moment—I was convinced at the time that this was final proof that I was, and would always be, alone in my times of greatest fear, and that I had no right to expect anything else.

But now we can move on, press play and leave this little interval of doubt and stunned fatigue, because it's time to push my son into the world, my spinning, squirming little bundle of muscle and limbs whose heart never once slowed as the waves of contractions washed over him. His father is back and the room is buzzing with movement and light. Here he is, crowning to Patsy Cline's "Walkin' after Midnight," the nurse and his father, who is holding my hand, both singing along quietly as I pause before bearing down again, and the midwife says, "Goot pooshes!" The cord wrapped twice around his neck, my body's last attempt to hold him, Sam trundles out with a jolt like train cars uncoupling and lets loose with the most beautiful, indignant, warbling yell I have ever heard.

My Plan, and all the stories and research woven into it, was in tatters on the floor, and despite the epidural, the lower half of my body felt like it had been savaged by a shark. I was two people, one destroyed and one built anew, and through the wreckage I could see two things: there was my husband next to me, blinking tears out of his eyes and laughing at the same time, and there, pink and raging with his tiny fists shaking the edges of his blue blanket, was my son. I reached for him and held him tight.

———

In his first few months, Sam cried. To anyone who's ever had a baby, or spent significant amounts of time around one, this statement is beyond obvious, like saying he breathed and drank milk and pooped. And if Stella was to be believed, he cried a great deal less than the average infant and was generally a content, alert, and mild-mannered baby. But the mitigating factor here was that the depression had come back for me, and since I had avoided taking my antidepressant for nine months of pregnancy and had never felt better in my life, I became even more convinced that if I were just disciplined enough, if I ate enough green leafy vegetables and drank enough water, I could will myself to stay in my mental lane and keep it together. I had to. Someone tiny and helpless depended on me, and my tandem parenting time was limited.

The news about Ross's acceptance to TOPGUN was still a month and a half away when Sam was born, and at that point, we were expecting Ross to go out on the boat for a month when Sam was a little less than two weeks old and then be home through December and January before leaving for Afghanistan. He would be gone for the next seven months, a giant, yawning stretch of calendar that I bulldozed over in my head with bright images of Sam getting ready to take his first steps and tottering over into his father's waiting arms. In September. In other words, I was thinking nearly a year ahead while I held a two-week-old baby whose face was still smooshed like a prizefighter's, and whose hoarse little cries of "lah, lah, lah!" regularly sent the blood thundering through my veins with the certain conviction that he was dying.

I had the best support system in the world. I know that now, and part of me knew it then. The squadron wives' club compiled a meal tree and brought delicious, home-cooked meals right to my

door every other night for two weeks. Ross was an active and he-
roic dad, whipping through diaper changes with the speed and
efficiency of a Formula One pit crew while I was still terrified of
Sam's circumcision and took eons to slather him with Vaseline.
My mother flew out from Texas and stayed for an entire month
while Ross left for the aircraft carrier. I pored over two wildly
conflicting books on infant care and sleep training, and she mer-
cifully kept turning down the volume on the baby monitor I carried with me everywhere. She cooked casseroles for the freezer
and insisted I have a beer and watch *Deadwood* with her on DVD,
and she routinely recited her own list of childcare mishaps, some
of which I knew she was exaggerating, just so she could make the
point that Doug and I survived and surely Sam would too.

That's how it looked from the outside, and that's how I prefer
to look at Sam's first few months of life when I retell it, because the
view from inside my head was awful. I heard him crying everywhere, in the white noise of the shower, in the rumble of my car's
tires over the road when I stepped out for a quick run to the convenience store, in the static on the silent baby monitor I was convinced was broken. When he cried, I was sure that he was looking
straight into my soul and seeing all the broken trash there, the
bent bicycle wheels, the rotting lumber, the stinking morass of my
corrupt and useless life that I somehow tricked everyone else into
not seeing. I was convinced that his cries were the hopeless wails
of someone who knew that fully half of his DNA was poison.

That was the bold, unfiltered flavor of crazy. The light version, and ironically the more harmful because it contained large
chunks of truth, was that he was a baby, and babies cry, but that I
should also stop and take a moment to reflect on the fact that I
had knowingly brought this tiny, perfect boy into the world only

to shepherd him through the same absurd dance of loss and long-ing I had spent my life hating. I would stop and look at him there on his changing table, his chin wobbling uncertainly, his onesie hiked up around his middle, and I would try to imagine finding the words to tell him, "I know you're sad, I know you miss him, but he loves you so much and misses you too, and he'll be home soon," knowing how lame "soon" would taste in my mouth, say-ing it to someone with no concept of time.

Four a.m. became the designated hour for semilucid mental wandering. While Sam nursed noisily and curled into a soft little ball against my chest, I would stroke the back of his upturned ear and let my exhausted mind drift. I thought a lot about his brain. On the third day of nonstop driving on our move out to Califor-nia, Ross and I had driven, separately, through Palm Springs, and I remembered the hills surrounding the city covered as far as the eye could see in wind turbines. It was a spectacular sight, and right then, as I watched the early morning sun touch each hill in succession against a backdrop of scudding thunderclouds, I de-cided it wouldn't be bad to retire on a windy stretch of land and forest the thing with wind turbines.

I imagined each of Sam's neurons as a wind turbine, and each austere blade as a dendrite, and then I pictured the dendrites festooned with white sparklers—a chemical signal flaring up in one place and then spreading like an ocean wave as the wind carried it to the next sparkler, the next blade, the next turbine, until you could see the path of the wind across the valley. I saw fingers of light, waves of it, rolling from one horizon to the other. Baby books encourage you to think this way when they emphasize over and over again how fast the beginning brain is, how nimble and plastic. His brain would never be this quick again. Unused turbines would disappear from the landscape, tipping over and rusting and returning to grass. As his mom, I was the wind, or at least part of it. I was responsible for stimulating him, feeding him, protecting his sleep, watching for signs of illness, and not turning him into a sociopath.

At moments like this, my energy flagging, the depression rising up and soaking me, I decided that, as a force of nature, I sucked. It's embarrassing to admit how far down the well I let myself sink before I asked for help.

The scene of the turning point makes my skin crawl, but it would be disingenuous to edit it out. It is of a quiet house at midnight, my mother newly gone, Sam sleeping but bound to wake up again in another forty-five minutes, Ross, newly home from work-ups and getting ready for bed, and me, ostensibly on a quick trip to the fridge for some water, crouched instead in a ball between the arm of a chair and the wall in our darkened living room. I was trying my best to hide, like when I was a kid playing hide-and-seek in the dark with my brother, and I'd picked a good spot to stop for a moment and quietly lose my mind. I tried to remember the lyrics to a Matisyahu song about asking Hashem for mercy and being thrown a rope. My eyes leaked tears and my arms and body shook with the effort of keeping all sound inside, especially the wobbly moan that kept trying to come out. I hadn't slept more than an hour at a time in weeks. When I did sleep, I had nightmares about losing Sam in the grocery store or the airport, or a strong gust of wind blowing him out of my arms and over a cliff, or wolves breaking into the house and eating him. My bones ached, my breasts were sore, and my hair was starting to fall out.

This is normal, I told myself, *this is normal, this is all hormones, suck it up.* I felt like a pressure cooker whose little counterweight was hissing and clattering and on the verge of spewing its contents all over the walls. I couldn't stop myself. In one awful, jittery burst of movement, I hacked repeatedly at my left inner forearm with the fingernails of my right hand until the flaring pain of the cuts crescendoed over all the other noise in my head and became one bright clear note of red.

The calm that followed lasted about two cool, silent minutes. Then the dread and the humiliation came (*Stupid, so adolescent!*), and I knew I'd have to find a way to bandage my arm, and that it would be hard to hide. I wished immediately that I could erase what I'd done. This is not a moment for the scrapbook. This is not a conversation you hope to have with your husband.

"Ross? I need to tell you something. I did something and I can't hide it and it was stupid. And I'm sorry. I wish I didn't have to tell you but I need you to hold me accountable for getting some help." *Accountable.* All the articulate words suddenly decided to show up when they were too late to do me any good.

"What? What did you do?"

"I may have . . . cut myself a little. It's stupid. It's this thing I used to do when I was younger. I'm not doing this very well." *Stupid, stupid, stupid.* I wanted us to skip over this part and just focus on the getting-help part.

"Doing what? What do you mean? You *cut* yourself?"

"Yes, okay? Being a mom. I'm not keeping my shit together. At all. I'm not holding it together right now." I wanted to hug him, I wanted to punch him, and I wanted this writhing, pinned-bug feeling of neediness and vulnerability to go away immediately. This was ugly and I hated that he was seeing it.

"Where is it? Let me see."

"*No.* Absolutely not. That's not important."

"Let me see it. Are you okay?"

I couldn't let him see it. Ross knew about my depression and had been wonderfully supportive over the years about helping me make sure I could get my antidepressant at each new duty station. He'd seen some crying jags and some wall staring, but nothing like this. *This is not fair to him,* I kept thinking, *to have to suddenly know how to deal with this.* But another voice, quieter, angrier, insisted, *This is not fair to me, to have to rely on other people for help, to try to explain myself when I'm at my absolute worst.*

That night I lay in bed, one of Ross's arms anchored across my stomach, and stared at the ceiling. I was coming to terms with an awful realization. It was so obvious: I'd spent all my time worrying about the wrong thing. In all the years leading up to having kids, I'd been focused on the logistics of a Navy career, the deployments, the moving, finding work and homes, and pulling the kids out of school over and over again. What I'd missed, what I should have been weighing, were the risks that came with my history of depression, both in terms of its effects on me as a parent and in the potential for passing it on to my children. What had I done? What kind of person was I? I felt like the answer to that was swelling and scabbing over on my forearm and all the bandages in the world couldn't hide it.

In the week that followed, I made an appointment with the midwife to get back on medication. The simple act of sitting in the waiting room, where I filled out a standard questionnaire on how I was recovering from childbirth and had to circle the 9 on the 1 to 10 scale for "Feelings of sadness or depression," was so excruciating that twice I nearly got up and left. By now, the sarcastic drill instructor in my head was on a near twenty-four-hour roll. *You fucking wimp, are you seriously about to cry again? Lock. It. Up.* It took one question in the midwife's gravely accented voice—"So! How are vee do-ink?"—for me to dissolve in sobs.

"Not so goot, eh?" she noted matter-of-factly as she got out the prescription pad. "Vell, das okay. It happens."

Here we were again: same medicine, same dosage. I was lucky, at least, for that, not to have to do the whole adjustment dance again—a little high, a little low, too much nervousness, not enough appetite, a chemical landing signals officer trying to talk down my wobbling brain—while caring for a newborn at the same time. Still, it felt like being handed the water wings that I couldn't seem to shed in the deep end of life, now with the added worry that I was passing incremental amounts of the medication to my baby through my breast milk. Again I took refuge in the suggestions of studies and the knowledge that, practically speaking, Sam was very clearly better off with the medicated me than the gibbering me hiding behind the furniture and cutting herself.

It took a while for the clouds to clear in my head, and while the medication did its work, I turned to the perplexing task of sleep training Sam by blending two completely opposed theories of parenting. On the one hand, I was reading about attachment parenting from Dr. Sears, and on the other, structured, scheduled feedings and naps that promised to make me "Babywise." Both were books given to me by other Navy wives, both came with warnings that the other side was nuts, and both offered dire diagnoses of how current cultural problems could be traced back to poor parenting in the earliest stages. I figured I could read everything and come out somewhere in between, but often when I heard Dr. Sears and the Babywise team squaring off in my head, it wasn't just two schools of thought about sleep training, it was the two warring halves of my heart—keep him close, so close, snuggled up to me at night breathing his sweet milky breath in little puffs near my shoulder and *never let him go*, versus lay him down in his crib, let him grump and cry himself to sleep a bit, drift off on his own terms, in his own bed, in his own room with the door closed and only the crackly little radio monitor connecting us.

Ross and I chose putting Sam in the crib, mostly on the advice of one haggard father who had just managed to extricate his nearly four-year-old son from the family bed with much crying and angst all around, but sometimes it felt like walking out into the middle of a field and laying my son down on a rock with the wind whistling around him and then walking away. It was that hard at first. I imagine most mothers feel some version of this when they negotiate the terms of sleep with their new babies, no matter what approach they take, but I couldn't help casting my mind out into a crazy loop of the future, like someone fly-fishing.

My thoughts snapped in a bright, improbable arc out over the sparkling eddies and I saw Sam all grown up, taller than me and giving me a quick, dismissive flip of a wave as he backed his beater car out of whatever driveway we were calling our own and peeled off for college or, God forbid, the military. Yale, the Navy, touring the country with some weirdo band—it was all the same, it was him leaving, and if I do things right, he will do this someday. He will leave, and I know it will feel familiar, the deepest echo of this ache of loss, the saddest, and somehow the proudest too, because I will have raised him to do this.

CHAPTER 17

Part of my mom's attempts to get my brother and me to ease back into our relationship with Dad after one of his work absences involved strategic disappearances. She would grab her purse one morning and announce that it was a "Dad Adventure Day" and to enjoy ourselves. The first few times she did this, I remember my dad looking just as uncomfortable as we did at the announcement, but soon we recognized the benefits to be reaped from this sudden tweak to the power structure. One was a complete disregard for how much sugar and salt we consumed, and another was a redefined notion of physical risk that opened all kinds of doors when it came to outdoor fun. One outing in particular has become part of my family lore, and I find myself thinking about it at the strangest moments.

It was summer and I was seven years old and Doug was six. We decided to make a day trip to San Marcos, where there was a great river for tubing. We stopped at a swimming hole near a bridge where the river widened before tipping smoothly over a containment wall and curving on downstream. Dad sat in the shade of some old pecan trees and started blowing up a couple of rafts while Doug and I waded out into the water in our life jackets.

"Be careful of the current," Dad said. "It gets stronger over next to that wall." I remember his words because they had the exact opposite effect he intended. There was suddenly nowhere else I wanted to be than the smooth, glassy curve where the water shone greenish before shattering into frothy white down the rocky side of the wall. Besides, a guy was already standing there, a brawny, muscle-shirted dude with sun-bleached hair and a tough-looking mustache, and the way he wheeled his free arm to keep his balance while the other clutched a Silver Bullet looked even more fun. I headed over, Doug paddling in my wake. The strange magnetism of the current tugging against my ankles and making my feet lose their grip on the rocks was electrifying, like a force I could fight against and win if I moved fast enough. I was completely absorbed in the effort, even at the point when I began to lose. I remember the next part in flashes—the sudden drop and water in my nose; the blue back of Doug's life jacket with its yellow belt, and the sun-browned hand of the man on the wall's edge grabbing Doug's belt and hoisting him clear; my continued fall and the unpleasant surprise that there were rocks underneath making all that water turn white, and broken glass; the second and even more unpleasant surprise that my life jacket could not hold my head above water and I was getting dunked in the current, once, twice, three times; and the panicked realization that the hardest I could kick, paddle, and fight did nothing to change the backward-speeding scenery on either side of the river. I couldn't get enough of a breath to scream, and soon it didn't matter anyway because I was around a bend and too far from any of the people who would have heard me.

It finally stopped when I got tangled up in a tree, slimy, bruised, bleeding, and coughing up river water through snot and tears. I pulled myself up and realized that the water was shallow enough for me to stand and had been for at least the last five hundred feet, which meant I could have saved myself a few of the last bruises by just putting my feet down. I caught my breath and climbed up the slippery bank, convinced that any minute now a crowd of horrified bystanders would come crashing through the trees calling my name. No one came. I began the hike back to the swimming hole, gradually getting more and more indignant at my nonexistent rescue party. Hadn't the guy with the mustache seen me go over? By the time I reached my dad, who was triumphantly holding aloft a fully inflated pink raft, I was fuming.

"Didn't you see that? I almost *died*!"

"Do what?"

"The waterfall? I fell down it! I almost drowned!"

"Oh! Well, didn't I tell you not to play there?"

I was so utterly enraged I just spluttered something at him and threw up my hands before stomping off to go pout under the pecan trees. In his defense, my dad knew these things about me: I was an excellent swimmer, a clever kid, and usually well behaved—rule-following to the point of being uptight. He had no reason to suspect I was also powerfully seduced, then as now, by acts of bravado meant to prove to the world how tough I was precisely because I felt anything but. I tried out several proclamations under my breath as I picked glass out of my shin.

"I will never again go in the water." As soon as I said it, I knew it wasn't true. "I hate my dad." Yes, but even that would probably end soon too. I sat for a while and let the breeze warm my back. Doug was still having fun. His raft was ready too and he was trying, and failing, to scrabble up on top of it with his life jacket in the way. My dad was floating in the water on his back with his eyes closed, slowly swishing his arms as his flexed white toes poked above the surface. I was back in the river within twenty minutes.

There are all kinds of ways to get too close to the edge of something that initially seems attractive but about which you actually know nothing. Along with his frequent-flyer miles and time logged away from home, my dad spent years amassing significant experience with crippling depression. Like his work and his mileage, I was aware of his depression really only in that it meant another absence, even though he was physically there. I never realized how close he'd gotten to a tipping point until he told me about it one afternoon when I was home from college, while we sat in the front seat of his pickup in the driveway. I don't remember where we had just been—it could have been something as boring as the grocery store—or how he brought it up, but I remember that even though the weather was chokingly hot, I felt rooted to my seat like I couldn't move.

"You two had just gotten on the bus to go to school and I got out the pistol. I sat on the side of my bed, and I just held it for a long time. I couldn't see a way for things to get any better, and I thought maybe Kathy and you and Doug would be better off without me."

"You did *what?*" He was quiet for a long time. "But I thought Mom got all the guns out."

"Those were just the shotguns. I guess I kept the pistol some-where else. Things were tough for a long time." If there's a correct way to react when your parent confesses to a suicidal period, even if it's far in the past, I don't know what it is. I just stared at him. "I'm not telling you this to scare you. I'm telling you because there are certain things in life that look like solutions, but they're not. If you give them too much thought, they kind of pull you to-ward them. You've got to be careful what you think about, espe-cially when it comes to depression."

By now, my dad and I were both on antidepressants and de-pression and its legacy in our family had become an open topic of conversation. Therapy had helped, as had my getting kicked out of school, but what really cemented the change in our family's treatment of the subject was my uncle Sandy's suicide a year after my expulsion. Sandy married my dad's older sister, and in so do-ing took on the role of de facto older brother and role model for most of the nearly four decades he and my dad knew each other. Sandy had worked in the oil field, and he and my aunt and my cousin had lived in Saudi Arabia for a short time many years be-fore us. I knew this, but it had seemed like random background information for most of the time I'd known them, like some weird vacation they took once. I could see, though, how the idea of mov-ing his family to the Middle East must have made much more sense to my dad the night he told us about it over dinner, and not like the wild pitch I saw it as.

Belatedly, and with a sick feeling of regret, I realized this meant my dad had been working from a pattern set by Sandy's stories, just as I would later find myself aping my own parents' steps. To be left guessing at how Sandy must have felt, even if only for a moment, on a sunny afternoon home alone with a gun in

Odessa, Texas—I could finally see, beyond my own experience, how depression affected, and continued to affect, my whole family. Perspective like this only lasts briefly, and the shock of it can take your breath away.

I think of my uncle and my father and the San Marcos River these days when I think about the irresistible pull of perfectionism and isolation I feel in times of great stress. I don't think it's a stretch to say I probably seek these situations out, just to prove something. Is idiocy like this passed down in the DNA? Or is it cultural, the result of too many cowboy shows and war movies, or of living in a male-dominated subculture with narrow female roles? What kind of world was I living in if asking for help was a weakness?

PART III

CHAPTER 18

TOPGUN. Always all caps, always one word.

If you belong to the tiny slice of the population who didn't witness Tom Cruise's career-making 1986 role as cocksure fighter pilot Lieutenant Pete "Maverick" Mitchell, grab yourself some light beer and cheese dip and fire up the Netflix. One would be hard-pressed to find another movie more chock-full of technical inaccuracies, reckless conflations of timeline, and puzzling homoerotic undertones, but in capturing the peculiar mix of old school manliness and mirrored-shades glamour in this subculture of the Navy, it's spot-on.

The way you end a year with no time is to meet it on its own level of absurdity, a *Dukes of Hazzard* handbrake turn where you switch gears from preparing for a deployment to Afghanistan and instead strap your four-month-old into his car seat and floor it across the Sierras by way of Lake Tahoe, streak out into the parched bottom of the Great Basin to Fallon, Nevada, "the Oasis of the Desert," to become part of an organization you know only from a movie, and whose name you have to keep following up to civilian friends and family with, "Yeah, it actually exists." Within the Navy community, I knew TOPGUN had a larger-than-life reputation, and that this was a game-changing move for Ross's career, but neither of us ever spoke of that. We had more pressing matters to attend to, like taking in a sobering, panoramic view of one of the worst-hit areas of the nation's housing crisis, and giving ourselves four days to find and put down an offer on the first house we'd ever bought.

I was ecstatic to have Ross home. The impending move, yet another new state where I knew no one, the swan dive into mortgage debt, the ridiculously short timeline in which it was all supposed to happen—none of this mattered, because there he was, my husband, my helper, Sam's dad, not gone. Lying next to him in bed one night, I told him I felt like I shouldn't hang around as much with the other wives in the squadron because I had my husband home and they didn't.

"It feels like hanging out with the Donner party, only I have this giant cake stashed away in my pack and they keep catching me with frosting on my face when we sit down together to talk about how we're starving."

Ross took it further. "It's more like an Airstream trailer you have, with a space heater and a microwave," he said, spooning me and tucking his hands down around my belly. " 'Hey, Rachel, could you help me fix this wagon wheel?' 'Um, yeah . . . it's just, my popcorn's almost ready.' "

We laughed like we were giggling in church, all wheezing and shaking, trying not to wake the baby or the dog, or disturb the cat, who had curled himself at our feet, but it was a sharp, painful laughter for me, the more intense for its tinge of guilt. I had him home. It was the best feeling, but I knew it was cold outside and would be for a long time yet.

TOPGUN is a special subset of pilots and aviation specialists within a special subset of pilots and aviation specialists. The larger entity is called NSAWC (pronounced "en-sock"), which stands for Naval Strike and Air Warfare Center. NSAWC as a whole consists of ten different groups, numbered N1 through N10, all representing various aspects of "excellence in naval aviation training and tactics development." This means excellence in personnel resources, intelligence, electronic warfare systems, and pretty much everything else even remotely related to carrier-based air warfare in the Navy. TOPGUN used to exist as its own entity, in Miramar, California (which is where Tom Cruise sulked around with his motorcycle in the movie), but a Base Realignment and Closure decision in 1993 moved the organization to Fallon, Nevada, an hour east of Reno and in the middle of the Great Basin and home to the Fallon Range Training Complex, some of the best flying real estate the Navy has, where it came under the NSAWC umbrella as the seventh N.

The purview of TOPGUN is essentially threefold: (1) they develop advanced tactics and recommendations for employment of strike fighter aircraft and their associated weapons systems in the fleet; (2) they teach a nearly ten-week course four times a year to train select strike fighter aircrew in the employment of tactics, and those who finish the course become strike fighter tactics instructors (SFTIs) for the rest of the fleet; and (3) each TOPGUN instructor is also a subject matter expert (SME) on a particular topic—anything from aircraft and weapons systems to hardware to employment of these elements to various aspects of whatever threat is currently under examination—and acts as the Navy's definitive voice on that topic.

A whole culture is associated with TOPGUN, with its own rules and traditions. The most serious of these concern the Patch. The Patch is the TOPGUN logo, but it's not just a logo. Besides being the visible declaration of association with TOPGUN, it carries the historical weight of the whole reason TOPGUN came into existence, which was due to the great number of pilots killed or captured in the early years of the Vietnam conflict. The Navy's air-to-air performance and combat kill ratio was troublingly poor, so it commissioned the now declassified Air-to-Air Missile System Capability Review, more commonly known as the Ault Report (for Captain Frank Ault, who conducted the review). The upshot was an evident need for consolidating and standardizing fighter expertise into some kind of advanced fighter weapons school. Hence, TOPGUN. It took me a year and a half to get all the backstory, but in this light, the organization's fanatical insistence on the importance of the Patch, the injunction against *ever* doing *anything* to dishonor, discredit, disrespect, or in any way call into question the reputation of the Patch, makes a little more sense. I originally thought it was an elitism thing, but above everything else, beyond all the hype and perception, it's a memorial and a commitment: "Never Again."

The Patch, simply as logo, is a white MiG-21 Fishbed in flight against a dark blue background. An orange gun reticle converges on the middle of its fuselage and a red ring surrounds the whole image, on which is written "United States Navy Fighter Weapons School." For as much as the name TOPGUN is invoked in the daily life of the organization, it appears nowhere on its most important image. The image itself has a hardworking life. Instructors wear it on the right shoulder of the flight suit and it appears as "fin flash" on the vertical stabilizer of every F/A-18 Hornet and F-16 Fighting Falcon NSAWC owns, but it also shows up embroidered, printed, etched, enameled, carved, painted, and otherwise emblazoned on a variety of items available for exclusive purchase: bumper stickers, T-shirts, sweaters, jackets, ball caps, baby blankets, onesies, earrings, pendants, key chains, shot glasses, beer pitchers, beer glasses, wineglasses, scotch glasses, Christmas ornaments, and anything else the instructors, or more often their wives, can think of. Over the course of our time in Fallon, I came to understand that there was a direct relationship between how ferociously hard instructors—and by default, their families—worked and how strong the urge became to accumulate items emblazoned with the Patch. Our own Patch collection is ridiculously large. Survival among this high-performance set seemed to come with a fanaticism for endurance and self-identification I'd previously seen only among marathoners.

The Patch also graces one side of a "challenge coin," which is about the size of a fifty-cent piece and bears the instructor's call sign and "TOPGUN Instructor" on the other. Challenge coins are not unique to TOPGUN—most other fleet squadrons produce them with their individual logos as well—nor is the tradition of taking it out at the bar and either slapping it down or tapping it against the table until everyone else presents their challenge coins as well, the idea being to stick the tab with the guy who showed up without his coin. But the adherence to this tradition, and the habit of former instructors and even retired ones to continue to carry their TOPGUN coin at all times, *just in case*, is unique.

The other major way to make a positive visual ID of a TOP-

GUN instructor, especially at a distance, is to check out what color T-shirt is visible at the unzipped throat of his flight suit. Light blue pegs an instructor. Just as the Patch never says "TOP-GUN," the powder blue never appears on the Patch. Similarly contrary is the issue of footwear. The aviation community has sought to differentiate itself from the rest of the Navy by wearing brown combat boots with flight suits rather than black ones, necessitating the shorthand phrases "brown shoe community" and "black shoe community." Yet another trademark differentiation among TOPGUN instructors is the insistence on black flight boots. Various stories exist to explain this choice, but there seems to be no official agreement on this score.

Finally, TOPGUN instructors even have a special word they use to identify each other: "Bro," as in "He's a good dude; he's a former Bro." It is used without a hint of irony.

All of these special traditions and visual markers are important because they are signposts that indicate you have gotten off onto a very different road within the Navy. They are the tip of the iceberg when it comes to how exactly TOPGUN differs from the rest of the fleet, and the rest is obscured, even from the wives.

There is much to learn for a TOPGUN wife, and it begins by assuming the role of "Murderboard widow." An instructor will spend most of his first year on staff learning, perfecting his knowledge of the assigned SME topic, and writing the lecture he will give, an hours-long speech given from memory with accompanying slides and critiqued, often brutally and in great detail, by the other instructors at a culminating event called a "Murderboard." The finest points—word pronunciation, body language, facial tics, how you press the key or hold the remote that changes the slides—come under review in the effort to make you into the perfect vehicle for the delivery of information. Total accuracy, complete clarity, zero distraction. Working on the lecture and preparing for the Murderboard consume a new instructor completely. Much of the lecture is classified information, so a wife can't even sit and listen to him practice and tell him if he's doing that head bob thing the senior Bros keep making fun of him for.

Many wives prepare impressive home-cooked spreads for the review committee on the day of their husbands' Murderboard. This is something of a tradition. From then on, they also provide potluck buffets for the evening "MiG Killer" lectures that take place once every three months as part of each TOPGUN class, where an experienced fighter pilot from some previous conflict comes in to share the story of his air-to-air victory.

As in the rest of the fleet, there is an officers' spouses' club, or OSC, for NSAWC, and it is open to all officers' spouses from N1 to N10, but there is also a TOPGUN spouses' support group (SSG). If you are a TOPGUN wife, it is possible to belong, and pay dues, to both, though what it is you're supposed to be doing with each group is at first confusing. To the best of my knowledge, the distinction is that the larger NSAWC OSC is recognized by the base legal office, and thus may hold fund-raisers, while the TOPGUN SSG is very careful to identify itself as a noncompeting "social support organization."

This is the scaffolding laid out for being a TOPGUN wife—the cyclical cooking duties, the continual production and sale of merchandise, the club within a club—but a lot happens in the liminal space. Keep in mind that Fallon has a population of just over three thousand and few employment opportunities. For me, it was the first time in my life since I was sixteen years old that I was totally and indefinitely unemployed. My job was now my family, and for someone accustomed to the feedback, identity, and remuneration of work outside the home, suddenly taking on the perplexing whims of an infant as your performance reviews and conflating the roles of "boss" and "husband" are easy—and costly—mistakes to make. The balance of power in our marriage had shifted once again. I no longer had the pressure valve of a job and a community outside of my role as a Navy wife, and without Stella and Jake around, no one within the tribe to help explain the rules to me in this new place.

Soon after our arrival in Fallon, I recognized the twin currents of extraordinarily high performance expectations and isolation. It was a feeling I was familiar with, enough to have formed my own sort of "Never Again." When it came time for me to go off to college, I had walked out of two separate campus tours at private universities known for their academics. They "smelled" like St. Stephen's, like jittery people winning at life but harboring ferocious private habits to compensate for the stress. Fallon, at first glance, felt suspiciously similar.

I didn't cook for Ross's Murderboard. That's the sound of hurdle number one smacking right into my knee. Instead, homesick and exhausted, Sam and I fled to Texas for two weeks. I often brought store-bought frozen lasagnas to MiG Killers, and I showed up to wives' club meetings unshowered and with chewed-up baby food on my shirt, which I scrubbed at furiously with a baby wipe in the seconds before I got out of my car. Hurdles two and three, smack, smack. Presenting what I considered a sane and competent face to the world was a project that kept getting put off for another day when Sam napped better or when our dog, who had suddenly developed diabetes, hadn't puked or peed all over the carpet again or when Ross was finally home to help out with some of the housework or figure out why the smoke alarms kept going off or why there was water building up in the crawlspace under the house. When that day arrived, then I could start having people over and work at forming some friendships. Until then, we were in triage mode.

A TOPGUN wife must also deal with the often-negative perception that comes from being associated with the club within a club. A wall exists, and it is built—sometimes accidentally and sometimes on purpose—by hands on both sides. Just as a largely inaccurate outside perception of elitism or snobbery follows her like a foul scent, so does her own idea of what she must live up to as an instructor's wife. The Patch, after all, casts a long shadow, and its inescapable presence can distort reality. In my case, it cast everyone else I met in association with TOPGUN in the honeyed light of utter perfection, and me, alone in a perfect, Patch-shaped shadow of Not Quite Measuring Up.

Buying a house before Ross had actually completed the course he was intended to instruct was a bit of a risk, one I worried made us look overconfident. Though the social divide between the wives of actual instructors and the wives of students slated to become instructors is actively spoken against in the TOPGUN SSG, it tends to get honored anyway. I told myself that the weeks, and then the months, I spent cloistered in the house mooning over my infant were temporary; that I was erring on the side of caution initially and that later I could find and hire sitters, make friends, get back to writing; and that as soon as I got caught up on some sleep and starting working out again I'd start to feel more human and less completely nuts.

Our first house. Every room, every window, every shelf, every closet, the play of light and shadow at every hour of the day and every season of the year, will likely remain burned into my memory for the rest of my life. I spent entirely too much time in my house. This was easy to do because it was obnoxiously beautiful, defiantly so in the face of everything that surrounded it. It was the kind of place we never would have been able to afford were it not for the housing crisis. The backyard alone made it hard to leave— every window across the back of the house gave out onto a carefully designed garden oasis with roses, lilac bushes, daylilies, wild primroses, juniper and cherry trees, and a little burbling stream fed by a circulating pump. According to the real estate agent, the whole thing had been designed by the previous couple when the wife began battling cancer, and I could see how nice it must have been, on days when she felt awful or exhausted, just to sit and watch the butterflies and birds that seemed to exist nowhere else in the windswept bleakness outside the fence.

Our house sat at the base of Rattlesnake Hill, directly across the street from the cemetery and separated from the funeral home next door by a thin irrigation canal. Through the living room windows and across the canal, I could see a parking lot full of mourners every couple of days and a periodic delivery of new caskets arriving by eighteen-wheeler. Our lot was a little spur hanging off of a proper neighborhood, and our house huddled with its back to the tidy, enclosed streets behind it, instead facing the (relatively) busy intersection of a road that looped around one side of Rattlesnake Hill to a dirt racing track and then around the other side to a small Paiute-Shoshone colony with its attached administrative offices, the local pound, the trap club, and a small civilian airstrip. The view out our front door was of headstones to the left and alfalfa to the right, with about fifty head of Black Angus cattle shuffling around in the winter, and a low range of bluish purple mountains beyond. At night, from the top of the hill, a white neon cross and a small stand of red-lit radio towers watched over it all.

By June, Ross had finished the class and embarked on his Murderboard preparation. Sam was nearly eleven months old. Ross and I had been on opposite schedules for nearly six months and had discovered something else about our house—it was possible to live together in it and rarely run into each other except in a few conflict zones, like the kitchen and the laundry room. I began to feel with an increasing keenness just how isolated we had become, both from a larger community of friends and from each other. I had met a few of the other wives, and had even had a couple over to the house, but without a job, proper sleep, or much regular adult contact beyond the checkers at Walmart, I found it almost impossible to come up with things to talk about. Instead, I listened. I heard just enough background on some of the running conflicts and history among and between the TOPGUN wives' group and the larger NSAWC OSC to become thoroughly intimidated by it all and convinced they would immediately out me as a fraud, and that any missteps I might make had the potential of torpedoing Ross's reputation and possibly his career. Default house arrest with an exemption for diaper runs didn't seem that bad in comparison, but luckily, we were fast approaching an opportunity for Ross and me to get out of town altogether, just the two of us, the first such opportunity in more than two years: a date to the Tailhook Convention.

Tailhook happens in Reno every year in September. Or rather, it does now. Before the 1991 sexual harassment scandal that made national headlines and cost many officers their careers, the convention took place in the logical choice for huge parties in Nevada, Las Vegas. Following the scandal, the Navy severed ties with the organization, and it did not restore them till 1999. Over the course of four days, carrier-based aviators, both active duty and retired, and their families, flock to Reno from all over the country. For a largely nomadic community, it marks one of the few occasions for a large-scale reunion, and aside from all the other business that takes place there—awards banquets, vendor presentations—it's widely seen as a giant party, a kind of bitter-sweet family reunion for a family that's always on the move and very familiar with "good-bye." There is a ton of booze.

Ross had been to Tailhook twice before without me and I was anxious to go. I desperately missed Stella and wanted to catch up with people we'd said good-bye to all along the way starting back in Pensacola. Maybe this was the healing experience of circular-ity I was looking for, the tying up of severed connections and the moment when I would slap my forehead and say, "*This* is why we love Navy life!" At the very least, I figured it was high time I did something social with the other TOPGUN wives.

Leaving Sam overnight for the first time was both physically wrenching and completely wonderful. My parents, weighed down with stuffed toys and storybooks, came out to visit and take care of him for the two days Ross and I would be in Reno. My mom seemed completely at ease with this task; my dad, perhaps sud-denly remembering the reality of those early years in Scotland, seemed as nervous as I was.

Ross and I had seen so little of each other in the preceding months as he prepared for his Murderboard that the conversation during the car trip to Reno, lacking the babbling of an eleven-month-old in the backseat, was halting and awkward. Eventually we left each other to our respective silences. I spent mine wondering how much time and distance would have changed the people I'd known over the past eight years, and how much they would see its changes in me. Did I look as exhausted and old as I felt? Would seeing old friends help Ross and me remember who we were when we started out? Were we happier then? Were we happy now?

I had no idea what he thought about.

I can only imagine what the Vegas version of Tailhook must have been like back in the days before the scandal, back before the beginning of the slow sea change in attitudes about women in the military and the vocal italics employed in the phrase "*today's* Navy," as in "That would never pass in *today's* Navy." I've heard this phrase said with both pride and chagrin. I had nothing to compare it to, but what I can remember of today's Tailhook was quite a good time. Once again departing from the rest of the fleet and its traditions, TOPGUN wives often designed and wore matching T-shirts and, wanting to fit in, I bought and wore mine. It seemed easier than having to come up with a cute cocktail dress and heels like the other wives at the convention, especially when everyone else, even the old-timers, wore flight suits.

Lots of events are planned around Tailhook, and most of them take place over a four-day period, but I gathered that most people really celebrate on only two nights. Friday night is for the flight suits and the squadron getups, for making laps around booths on the hotel convention floor, and then for cruising a circuit of "admins," smaller meeting rooms rented out by individual squadrons and stuffed to the gills with fancy liquor and pounding music. Saturday night is for going out on the town with friends, for wading through the peculiar mix of grit and glitz that is Reno, and for an exhausting number of "chance" encounters with Navy folks in their civilian clothes because, in reality, we all pretty much go to the same places.

On Friday night, I wore my TOPGUN Wife shirt, accidentally dropped my phone in the toilet, and spent most of the night looking for Stella and other friends I'd lost touch with outside of Facebook and not finding them. Ross and I spent Saturday subdued with hangovers in a little TOPGUN clot by the pool, but by evening, we had recovered and were looking for adventure. The early part of the evening was frittered away on cab rides back and forth across town, again trying to figure out where we belonged and with whom and not agreeing. Finally, Ross and Jake got in touch and arranged a time for us all to meet up with Stella and her sister and brother-in-law, also a Navy pilot, who were in from the East Coast. We ended up finding what looked like a tiny country and western bar hidden way back in the corner of the hotel, a giant, mirror-covered boot glittering over the dance floor. It was sparsely populated. Our group of six was the only Navy presence.

Stella and I hadn't talked much in the year I'd been gone, apart from a few scattered text messages, though she and her kids had been on my mind pretty much constantly. She was busy with a new consulting venture that relied heavily on recruiting a network of military wives, and at first she seemed "on" and connected in a way that made me feel small and boring, holed up in the boonies with my baby and a husband who was never home. But the more we talked, the more I just let it all out. With Stella, I wasn't afraid to say that I was a mess, or that I was afraid my writing would never amount to anything, or that I didn't have any friends. I missed her terribly and told her so.

"Don't worry—it's hard when your kids are babies, but it gets better. And you'll make friends. You're my Roxy, God damn it," she said, referring to my nickname from our drinking days during deployment. "Show them all how awesome you are."

By the end of the night I had resolved to find my footing in Fallon. I had found Jessie before and I had found Stella. I could find other friends if I looked hard enough. After all, we finally had the Murderboard behind us and Sam was close to being fully weaned. In another couple of months he could be walking, and then, who knew? Maybe Ross would be home more, maybe I could have some time to myself, get back to writing, and regain a sense of who I was outside of an exhausted mother and subpar housewife. This alienated, off-balance feeling was all in my head, a holdover from the bout of postpartum depression and my fluctuating hormones from coming off breastfeeding. Time to shake it off and get my head back in the game.

The DJ switched from country standards to old Michael Jackson songs and I strutted out on dance floor, vodka confident. I love to dance, and as I shook the stiffness from my muscles and felt the beat drown out all the chatter in my head, old feelings of freedom and possibility started to come back. A stranger appeared out of nowhere, a young man in a fedora who squared off in front of me and initiated the first honest-to-God dance battle I'd ever been in. Heart pounding and covered in sweat, I eventually conceded to him, but I felt lit up and visible in a way that I hadn't in years. By now, the floor was filling up with people and we danced—Stella and I, Jake and I, Stella and Ross, all of us together, and finally Ross and I, his grip on my hands and waist strong and forceful, as if at last we remembered who we were.

CHAPTER 19

Back in Fallon five months after Tailhook, I was sitting on the floor of the bathroom weeping into a bright yellow hand towel while Sam sat chest deep in bubbles and whacked away at his Fridge Farm and Ross put a tray of wedge french fries into the oven. Periodically, I leaned forward and retched into the toilet bowl, a move Sam watched with interest before going back to his whacking, only now with the added sound effect of his own version of my gagging and moaning. The imitation was one he had perfected from mornings in his high chair as he watched me scrambling eggs and then lurching to the kitchen sink. He'd even learned to top it off with an "oh, God." That evening, however, I was unable to give him the usual weak smile and say, "Thanks, buddy." I was pregnant again, the result of the night we'd been on the dance floor, and the morning sickness this time around was much worse and continuing well into my second trimester.

On that particular evening, I was holding three facts in my head, and their overlapping borders were emitting a toxic funk that made it hard to concentrate. First, my children were going to be twenty months apart, just as my brother and I were nineteen months apart, meaning I had replicated not one but two of what I considered to be my mother's more questionable choices (the first being marrying a man who works a dangerous job requiring him to be gone a lot). Second, it was now January 2012 and our decision about whether or not to stay in the Navy after Ross's commitment was up was fast approaching. My hoped-for revelation about how I could embrace military life had so far not shown up, while Ross openly spoke of hitting the twenty-year retirement mark. Third and finally, that old feeling was back, the depression, underneath the fatigue and the nausea, not just a little bit of "the blues" but the Real Thing, the big black cloud with its landscape-altering storms in tow.

More than anything, the return of the depression had me spooked. I hadn't taken antidepressants when I was pregnant the first time because there had never been a need. I had assumed this time would be the same, and that I'd have a leg up knowing that I should be vigilant in the weeks following birth. Every visit with my obstetrician so far had been completely routine, so much so that I had begun feeling guilty even considering bringing up the issue of persistent, crushing sadness and apocalyptic thoughts with no identifiable source. I sat outside myself in the waiting room and looked at the other mothers, many of them teenagers, some struggling to work out advance payment plans for their deliveries, and thought, *Who am I to be sad with my beautiful, healthy son and my husband with a job that pays for my care? Who am I to feel lost and lonely and worried that I won't be able to cope?*

I had been tending a few green shoots of friendships, and one was with Diane, an architect from the Midwest who had a quiet voice and an earnest way of cutting to the emotional heart of a conversation. She had two young children as well and was working from home for a firm out of state. I felt comfortable confessing to her that I was doing something as potentially delusional as writing a book, and we found a lot to talk about in the struggles of parenting toddlers while trying to carve out time and space to do creative work. I took solace in the book club Diane invited me to join, a group that limited itself to ten members and extended invitations to new people only when someone else relocated. I'd heard it referred to among other wives, mockingly, as "the super exclusive book club," and when I heard that it was also standard practice among the group to rotate hostess duties for a sit-down dinner as part of the meetings, I figured I'd never get in. But then one of the members moved to Japan and Diane put my name forward and no one balked, so I figured it was finally time for me to learn how to host a decent dinner. All the members were military wives, but only a few were from TOPGUN, meaning we all had common ground, but not enough for the meetings to wander too far into shop talk or gossip. We actually stuck to the book and our conversations were lively and long. For me, it was like a welcome return to the days of grad school, and those nights we spent unraveling narratives and spinning connections between our own lives were often one of the only things keeping me afloat.

After more than a year in Fallon, I found another friend, Mikayla. She had just moved into the house behind mine and was having withdrawal from leaving her East Coast job as a hospital administrator. Mikayla was skeptical of wives' clubs and rolled her eyes at a lot of the TOPGUN hype, which made me like her immediately. She also had a habit of using casually affectionate nicknames for everybody, like "buddy," "homey," and "friend." It reminded me of Stella and of my days as Roxy. When Mikayla got pregnant with her first baby a few months after I'd gotten pregnant with my second, I envisioned us turning into the kind of best friends who would raise their babies together—we even talked about how nice it would be to cut a hole in the back fence to make it easier to pass back and forth between each other's houses.

In January, about four months after I met Mikayla, I convinced her to come to her first TOPGUN SSG meeting with me. I was having a rare burst of energy and hopefulness and had decided that if I went to more of the scheduled social events, I might be able to beat back the darkness gathering in my head. Once there, we watched, glumly sober and pregnant, as everyone else enjoyed Mardi Gras–themed appetizers and industrial-strength hurricane cocktails. Sadly, not even stone-cold sobriety was any help to us in figuring out why the evening ended the way it did. Somehow the meeting's agenda devolved into misunderstandings, failed attempts at clarification, even greater confusion as old grievances joined the mix, and then a perfect storm of shouts and tears and scattered exits. When we finally managed to extricate ourselves, Mikayla sat in the front seat of my car for a stunned beat before she laughed and said, "What *the fuck* was that?"

"Dude," I said, "I don't even know." What I should have taken from the experience was a comforting affirmation that perhaps I wasn't the only one who was feeling a little stressed out by playing the role of a TOPGUN wife. Instead, I concluded that there were forces at work way beyond my understanding and that the wisest strategy was to withdraw again. I needed to get my own mental house in order—the last thing any of us needed was more drama.

February passed and I sank lower. Weekends were now for

catching up on all the things that had built up during a week of near total absence from Ross and my own inadequate household management efforts while sick, pregnant, and chasing an infant. Everything tied us to the house—Sam, my crushing fatigue, our diabetic dog who needed twice daily insulin shots and careful monitoring of her blood sugar, our strained bank account preparing for another baby with one still in diapers, a million small chores that never seemed to get done fast enough or "the right way."

Ross was under pressure at work for a complex situation about which he could tell me next to nothing, except that government figures many, many pay grades above him were involved. For nearly a month, the only way we discussed his work was for me to ask him, "How was your day?" and for him to reply, "Bad. Again." He seethed and glowered at me over the snowdrifts of unfolded laundry collecting on the couch, the absence of meals, the state of the countertops and kitchen sink, the grocery bill, the level of the thermostat. He had never nitpicked me before about how or whether I cleaned and maintained things at home—it was one of the things I loved about him from when we were dating, that he wasn't a slob and that he was just as ready and willing to pick up a scrub brush as I was—but now that I was home all the time pregnant and caring for Sam, suddenly I was getting detailed instructions and critiques of the order in which I did things and the products and techniques I used. I finally snapped at him that he was Murderboarding me. He shot back that he felt like he was failing at everything, both at work and at home.

Initially I confided some of this to Diane and Mikayla, but pretty soon I grew tired of the sound of my own voice, of the same complaints repeating themselves week after week. I started taking long drives with Sam on the highways outside of town because I found it was often the only way I could make sure he was properly supervised and also hide my face from him so I could weep. Our family went to a Methodist church briefly during this period, part of a crisis-containment decision on both of our parts to seek some kind of counseling. The pastor was kind and helpful and recommended a marriage counselor who was neither, but instead of admitting that the match with the counselor was a bad fit and finding another, we just stopped going. I became preoccupied with the fear that whatever toxic mess was building up inside me, and between Ross and me, not only was it evident to everyone we met, but also I might be spreading it every time I shook hands with people in the "pass the peace" part of the church service. We stopped going to that too.

It's called "sniveling" in the Navy when you put in a request not to be on the schedule for a particular time slot for whatever reason—a doctor's appointment, family needs. When it came to marriage counseling neither of us was ready to "snivel," to make the necessary logistical sacrifices for a sitter and time off work. We both believed that time could still make things better—my pregnancy, his work situation, Sam getting a bit older—maybe it would all look different in a couple of months if we just gritted our teeth and toughed it out. For my part, the horror of exposure still held on from my boarding school days. After being kicked out of St. Stephen's and barely finishing up my tenth grade year in public school, I'd made one last, brief trip to Saudi Arabia, where my brother was still finishing up the ninth grade. I'd spent most of my two-week trip afraid everyone was talking about me and staying mostly in my room, either reading or hanging out with Larry. I had just about convinced myself that I was being paranoid, and had agreed to spend an afternoon with Larry and some other friends at the company pool, when a girl, young enough to still be a little swaybacked, walked over to my lounge chair and said flatly, "I heard you got kicked out of school." I was too stunned to answer. Fallon in general, and TOPGUN in particular, felt like communities just small enough to be similarly aware of, and interested in, scandal.

Added to the load we were carrying was Ross's father's rapidly failing health. I was close to my father-in-law, and the long, slow road of his battle with Alzheimer's had been devastating. Ross and I had different ways of dealing with Danny's illness—I wanted to talk about it, go home at every opportunity, and try with every visit to believe in a plateau in the disease's course or some flash of recognition that may or may not have been real. Ross wanted to preserve, whole and unaltered, his much more extensive memories of his father in the prime of his life, the many camping trips they'd taken together, the deep and abiding connection he'd established at a time in his teenage years when I was actively shoving my own parents away. Key to the success of his strategy was *not* talking about Danny, unless it was a brief story from before his diagnosis, some fond and funny recollection that always broke off short with a long silence in its wake. From the beginning of our relationship, I had worried that the death of his father, especially if we continued to not talk about it, would trigger some sort of breakdown in him. To Ross, who was about to be a new father twice over in rapid succession, and who was learning to fill the role while working the most demanding job of his life, discussing his feelings about losing his dad was pointless and cruel.

So we both grieved, and this also made it easy for me to lose track of the line between legitimate sadness and my diagnosed illness. I started thinking that maybe "depression" was just shorthand for "a removal from all things and all people, and a certainty that if there is a God, He is far from me and cannot help." I knew better, but in the moments where I couldn't find the old standbys that had gotten me through before, the phrases "this is not permanent" and "this is not all I am," along with the new one, "I am someone's mother," an idea was beginning to form about how strong the garage door tracks might be, and how easily the nylon ropes we used to tie down furniture in the pickup for moves might be repurposed.

By the first week in March I had stopped sleeping. On March 5, I walked into my OB's office without an appointment and with Sam on my hip and said flatly to the woman at the window, "I need help." I must have looked as awful as I felt because she didn't even ask me to sit down, and instead kept her eyes on me as she called out down the hall behind her, "Doc?" My doctor reviewed the risks of antidepressants in pregnancy with me, but also said that by the third trimester, "most of the major structures are already in place." Then, perhaps trying to lighten the mood a bit as he got out his prescription pad, he asked, "You're not thinking of jumping off a bridge, are you?" "No good ones in town," I said, and watched as his hand paused.

I remember the date because I was seven months pregnant and about to see a jet crash.

CHAPTER 20

It's the thing we all think about but don't say. It's the reason wives' clubs have call trees and everyone fills out paperwork on how to get in touch quickly through multiple avenues. It's the reason there are so many documented and explicit emergency procedures to memorize and follow. I would argue that it's the shadow that lies right under the whole idea of aviation, which is itself a cunning and temporary suspension of the rules of physics. A crash is the bottom line I am thinking of when I worry that Ross hasn't had enough sleep, or that I'm distracting him from more important things if we have a fight, or it's past the time he should be home and I haven't heard from him. It's what I think of when the phone rings when I'm not expecting it, or there's a knock at the door and a car I don't recognize in my driveway, or there's a bunch of sirens and a column of smoke in the sky outside. In other words, I think about it often and automatically, but it's a compromise I made so long ago that it blends into the background of life, like the ever-present jet noise.

It all used to be an abstract sort of nightmare to me. Crashes happened, accidents in training, but they were at other airfields. Ross knew some guys who died, but he didn't know them well. I watched the news coverage, read their official bios, and looked at their squadron photos—Ross's latest official photo sat in a small frame on Sam's dresser so we could say good night to it when he was away—and prayed for their families. They were like shock waves, impacts that rocked us but didn't touch us.

I used to do a terrifying sort of math in the time between when I knew there had been an "incident" and when I finally got the official story about what had happened and to whom. I thought of Ross, but only briefly. I can't explain it, but it's something like checking to see if your leg's still there—you do it once, just because, but you never expect to find it missing because surely you would have felt it already. Then I would think of all the pilots I knew whose schedules put them in range of the current disaster and I would methodically eliminate each one from the target zone by imagining them as I last saw them, imagining their families, and imagining some point in the future that they had to be around for—the next cookout, the next squadron costume party, the next little kid birthday party. If I imagined hard enough, somehow someone I knew wouldn't end up in the final version of the equation. It always worked, but it was an awful way to be thankful.

Then on March 6, 2012, the morning after I'd walked into my OB's office and asked for help, I saw a jet plow into the earth two hundred yards from my car as Sam and I were heading to the base clinic for a doctor's appointment for Sam's cough. Everything about the day was off, including the fact that I was running early for the appointment. Spring had arrived and the day before was sunny and clear, as it would be the very next day, but on that particular morning snow and ice pellets shot horizontally across the road in a brutal wind that buffeted my car and made me tighten my grip on the steering wheel. Sam, sixteen months old, babbled and kicked restlessly in his backward-facing car seat.

At a little before 9:15 in the morning, I turned onto the road that led to the base. A runway ran alongside the road at a roughly forty-five-degree angle. Right after I made the turn, a jet swooped in above me, much too low. It pointed its tail right at me as it skidded into a turn to the south to face the runway. The wind was coming strong from the north and blowing snow and dirt across the road, so I knew the pilot was fighting it, that it was shoving him down from behind. The jet was small, with one fin and a single exhaust nozzle. That's how I knew it wasn't Ross, though he was scheduled to fly later that morning. These are all things I knew right then, but as the jet made the turn and we started moving together in the same direction, his back end started to sink. He was still going too fast, and the snow and wind were coming down in between us. I had never seen anybody come in for a landing at this particular runway, so I was unsure as I watched through the driver's side window where the runway started or how close the jet was to reaching it.

It looked like a hand was shoving him down and I knew he was too fast and too low and I started to say "oh, no." His engines roared as he tried to add power, and then his back right end hit and there was a flash of orange as it caught fire. I started to scream. A wall of dirt and smoke went up and we both kept going, moving in the same direction like we were locked together somehow in this thing that couldn't be happening. I put on the brakes and heard myself saying, *No, no, no,* and *Oh God oh God somebody help him get out get out get out,* and then *God help him, God please help him.*

The mind knows things before we want it to.

I never saw a seat eject, and as we both came to a stop, I saw him clearly again, just past trees that were winter bare. The cockpit was on fire and the flames were at least ten feet tall, the only color in a landscape of white static and black tree trunks. All the fire went to the front of the plane and I remember wondering why that was so, why it wasn't only the back end where it had hit the ground.

A black pickup truck raced from behind me to a set of chained-shut gates in the fence separating the base from the road, and a man in jeans and a sweatshirt jumped out and climbed the fence, concertina wire and all, and ran toward the plane. I had a wild hope that he knew about some trigger on the outside of the cockpit that could eject the pilot, but as he got closer it became clear that the fire was too big. He stopped running about fifteen or twenty yards from the plane and paced back and forth, raking his hands through his hair. Other cars stopped along the road with me—a blue and white Jeep, another dark pickup with a maroon electric wheelchair gathering snow on a hitch on the back, and a gray pickup behind me. An old, slim, balding guy in a white shirt and jeans got out of the gray truck and started taking pictures. In the middle of my crying I yelled that he shouldn't be doing that, but my windows were up so he didn't hear me. The wind shook the car gently and snow and dirt crackled against the back window. I put my hand against the glass of the driver's side window and the heat from my fingers left a hand-shaped fog impression. Sam was silent in the backseat.

Between two and five minutes passed, and some of the

stopped cars pulled away and started down the road, so I followed. I went to the front entrance gates, and the drivers ahead of me seemed to be moving through them fast without saying anything to the man on duty. I stopped and told the gate guard, who had crooked teeth and braces with little blue bands on them, that a plane had gone down in the field and I didn't know what I should do. I was crying and he asked me to repeat it; then he said, "Wait one," and stepped into the gatehouse, and another guard came out with him. I repeated myself, and he grabbed his walkie-talkie and told me to pull aside and wait. Still no sirens. Then he came back and said the right people knew about it and it was being taken care of, so I went on to the clinic for Sam's doctor's appointment.

At the clinic, I pulled in and found a parking place and got out into the driving wind and snow. I could smell something, part burning, part plastic, and as I rounded the corner of the car to get Sam, I heard a weird muffled sound, half poof, half pop, and I wondered if it was an explosion, maybe a belated ejection. It sounded like all the air being let out of something. I checked in at the front desk like normal and wondered again if I should say anything. The lady at the desk told me we were neighbors, that she had seen Ross and me out walking on Sunday, and I said, "Hi, neighbor," and was shocked and a little disgusted at how normal I sounded, though I knew I looked like hell.

Sam and I went to sit in the waiting room. I set him down to play with the puzzles laid out on a small table, but he stood watching me uncertainly. I tried to smile at him. He came back over to me and sat quietly in my lap, alternately leaning his head against my chest and then leaning back to stare up at my face, for the next seven minutes until we were called. It seemed very important to keep track of the time, and I was disturbed by how gummy it seemed—like three minutes would snap by and then the next three would stretch out in a rubbery infinity so improbable that I checked the face of my phone to make sure the wall clock wasn't broken.

During that time I noticed people starting to cross the lobby and leave their desks, grabbing purses and really colorful lunch coolers that looked weird against their dark blue camo uniforms. Lots of people seemed to have a place to go. I saw a doctor buttoning up his white coat and walking fast from window to window. Two guys on the couch near me seemed to understand what was happening. I looked at the clock and it was 9:25. I felt like I might throw up, and it felt like I was getting period cramps. I worried about the baby and held Sam tight. I closed my eyes and leaned my forehead down against his and said a prayer.

My favorite corpsman came and got us, a thoroughly professional guy with glasses who looked very young. He apologized in advance if it seemed like he was rushing us through the intake, but, he said, they wanted to stay on schedule. He was very calm. He measured Sam's head, left the height the same from the last time we'd visited the doctor, and plunked him fully clothed on the little floor scale. Nineteen-inch head, 31.65 inches tall, 21.02 pounds.

I can remember these things, but not if I ever saw landing gear, and not that the plane hit a low building and that was where it came to rest and burst into flames, and that it never even made it to the runway. I remember how loud it seemed as it got closer and closer to the ground, and how weird its placement in the sky was, how I was shocked at what it was doing and watched it the whole time, right into the ground, and how I watched it burn, crying and yelling for someone to help the pilot while I did nothing. I yelled until I felt my pinkies losing sensation, which meant I was hyperventilating, but my voice did nothing, stopped nothing, changed nothing.

What my mind knew that I didn't want it to know was that a man had left the world right in front of me. The official policy following a crash is silence—no phone calls, no texts, absolutely no Facebook. Silence allows the grim rituals space to work— securing the scene, coordinating emergency workers, notifying the next of kin. What do you do on a morning like this, having seen the event take place? You fill the prescription, you go home, you make lunch for your son. You set the ring volume on your phone to max and check the battery level again and again. You fight the fear that despite what you know—small jet, one fin, one exhaust nozzle, your husband scheduled for a flight that shouldn't have taken off yet—you will somehow get blindsided. You wait. And when the call finally comes, the one where you hear his voice and he says he's okay, you listen to all the other facts, including which husbands of friends had also been up in the air, fighting the weather and being redirected to other fields, before you finally say, "I saw it happen." The relief is still a long way off when he says, "Hold tight, I'm coming home." You won't actually feel it until he walks in the door and you bury your face in his shoulder and let the snowflakes melt against your skin.

It was only from this distance that I could ask, "Was it anyone we knew?"

"You never met him. He was a contractor flying as an adversary. It wasn't a Navy plane, but he used to be in the Navy."

"Did you know him?"

"Yes." A long pause. "I had to call his boss and tell him and—" Ross stopped, and I looked up at him. His eyes were welling up and he reached up to pinch the tears out one-handed.

Mikayla came over then, windblown and coatless, having run out her front door and along the canal road when she heard from another wife that I'd witnessed the crash. She hugged me once, hard, and said, "I love you," then ducked out quickly when she saw Ross had come home. We stayed this way for the rest of the afternoon, not talking much but staying close to each other, huddled inside as the storm blew itself out.

The question of how long it took, which of those impossibly stretchy awful seconds was the pilot's last, lay like a giant crack underneath everything I did from the moment his plane hit the ground until many weeks, months, even a year later. Time, time had to be accounted for, so much so that I wrote out a timeline as soon as I got home from the base and as many facts as I could remember and swear to, and I wrote them all down in a list, convinced that I should be ready when someone called needing to know something. I could then hand over my list and maybe it would fit into some larger picture whose unbalanced part could then be found and isolated: here's why it happened, here's how it will never, ever happen again. But the call never came and the question of time began to bother me in a different way. What was the last thing he saw? What was his last thought?

So much of writing for me is going back over moments where I can remember my part, imagine someone else's, and then check with that person and see what it really looked like from their angle and tease out all the nuances that got lost in translation. It's a way of discovering the exact distance between myself and other people, especially the ones I love. But with the crash, I was stuck in my car, behind a chain-link fence and some trees with the radio playing some song I'll never remember. One of my sons was strapped in his car seat facing backward into an unforgiving wind of snow and dirt, and the other was trapped inside me listening to muffled screams and awash in cortisol and adrenaline. And the man leaving the world was stuck inside his jet.

Can we shape a moment like that with our minds and with the story we tell ourselves after the fact? Is that maybe even allowed as a kind of grace, since the worst, a man's death, has so clearly already happened? If so, then I say this:

He died on impact. His last image was of snowflakes. His last thought was of his family.

For a long time following the crash, I was like a sleepwalker. I moved, stunned, from one task to the next, marveling at small details as they floated past me, disjointed and disconnected, trying to decide if each detail was meaningless or deeply significant. I didn't sleep much. I had always considered it a figure of speech when people said they couldn't get an image out of their minds, or kept seeing something happen over and over every time they closed their eyes, but I learned that this is actually true. The mind snags. The film jumps the reel and the same sequence repeats itself ad nauseam. For me it was four frames that moved in halting succession: the jet too low, the back end of the right wing hitting the ground and flashing orange, black tree trunks and a wall of dirt and snow, and the jet at rest blooming fire. One, two, three, four; one, two, three, four.

Every now and then an urgent question would present itself, some detail that seemed like the key to understanding what had happened and why, or some alternate scenario for how things could have gone, and I needed Ross to tell me right then, as precisely as possible, everything he knew about what I was asking. He was patient with this. I asked about ice on wing surfaces and fuel readings and how the wind pushes on a plane in flight. I asked about emergency landings and ejections and radio calls and where exactly each runway begins and ends. I woke up in a sweat the first night, sick to my stomach with this question: If I hadn't been there on the road, in the way, could he have landed on the pavement just outside the fence? No, Ross said, that's not ever something they train for when they consider emergency landings because there's the risk of power lines or other obstructions and a road is just too small. I wanted to believe him, but it took me a while to accept this.

What I didn't ask about at first, what I couldn't bear, was anything about the pilot. I knew only that he was someone Ross knew and had worked with and liked, but someone I had not yet met. I was careful to use only impersonal pronouns in reference to the pilot when asking Ross about this or that procedure or decision. It seemed deeply wrong, like an unforgivable breach of etiquette approaching the level of sin, to learn someone's name only after seeing something as intimate and precious as his last moments.

The weekend directly after the crash was the TOPGUN "Dining Out." A Dining Out is a major social event in any squadron and usually takes place either once a year or once every couple of years; it is highly structured with traditions, toasts, drinking games, and all sorts of rules, and it was exactly the kind of thing I suddenly wanted to avoid completely, but it was also something that I understood was now entirely necessary. Collectively, the TOPGUN staff needed something to ram it back into gear, quickly, and since this event had been planned far in advance, the logical choice was to press on. So my mom flew out as planned to stay with Sam, and Ross and I packed up for a night in Lake Tahoe. He prepared his Dinner Dress Blues and I swapped the form-fitting siren red dress I'd been planning to wear for a long, shapeless black one that reminded me—comfortingly in this instance—of the *abayas* I'd seen Saudi women wear. I could think of nothing more enticing at that point than the possibility of moving through the evening in a column of shadow and blending in so thoroughly that I could pretend I was Photoshopping myself out entirely. In a small gesture of remembrance, I bought a few stems of white orchids and Mikayla and I pinned them in our hair. I layered concealer over the reddish purple circles under my eyes and crammed my purse full of tissues just in case I had to duck into a restroom and lose it.

The celebration seemed subdued, and as much as I felt a little tender about the idea of applauding naval aviation, the company of a bunch of people who knew what had happened and were also struggling to make sense of it was comforting. We didn't talk about the crash much, and for my part, I was relieved that loud music and crowded tables provided a little cover for me to grapple with how strange it felt to be tottering around a casino, pregnant and in heels, with a bunch of people in Dress Blues. Luckily, everyone else seemed to be in costume too. We passed bachelor-ettes with condoms stapled to their veils and braying men in Hawaiian shirts and finally ended the evening in a club where an angry-looking girl in thigh-high boots, fishnet stockings, tiny little briefs, and a bustier stomped back and forth on a catwalk above the dance floor. Our group VIP booth had an iced bucket of champagne and a pyramid of stamp-sized brownies. I felt like I was in the wrong movie.

It was Mikayla who came up with a way of getting around my persistent block in talking about the pilot when she suggested very gently that I take a look at his blog, which took its name from his call sign. A call sign, in this case, meant everything to me—it was a handle that was at once deeply personal but also one step removed from how his family might have thought of him. With a call sign, I could touch lightly around the idea of who he was and what it felt like to meet him only after his death. I could read his posts and hear a voice in his writing that was simultaneously familiar and strange in its technical expertise and deeply romantic in its descriptions of flying. I could read the outpouring of grief in the comments left and feel like the weight of all that sorrow was somehow buoying me and shaping all of my unspoken panic and shock and sickness into something that made a little more sense. *This is awful*, it said. *This is awful, but this is what happened.*

Holding on to a call sign first and then using it to pull myself slowly and tentatively closer to learning about the man whose death I witnessed allowed me to tread lightly around the fear I had grown up with, that one day I would find out very impersonally, on the news most likely, that my father's rig had caught fire and that he was never coming home. It allowed me to hold my breath and edge just past the nearly identical fear that I now found myself married to.

It was important for me to read this man's words and the comments of the scores of people who wrote in to his blog because it gave me back my faith in words, that even though they didn't have the power to hold a plane aloft or weaken the wind or move the fuel needles up a bit, maybe they could map the terrain of grief that surrounded the crash and help us all feel a little less lost in the middle of it. I also took great comfort in the skill and elegance of the pilot's sentences and the fact that I could lever myself up out of my sleepless bed and bring them up on my screen even in the middle of the night, even after it had finally begun to sink in that he was really gone. Finally, reading his words gave me some kind of hope that if I just kept looking, maybe I could find my own words again, and maybe if I were careful, and honest, and respectful, I could build some kind of small memorial to this other writer out of the moment our lives intersected, and how that moment changed my life forever.

The more I learned about the crash—and that was very little, since it was under investigation by the National Transportation Safety Board and the process is very slow and methodical—the more it seemed like nothing could have been done to prevent it and I struggled to put a name to how I felt about it. The pilot's skills were second to none. The controllers had done nothing wrong. The jet had not malfunctioned. The weather—the *weather*— had simply changed too suddenly, and the pilot had been unable to land at Fallon and was rerouted to Reno, but then the airfield at Reno had closed before he'd gotten there so he'd had to turn back around and try to make it back to Fallon. The visibility and winds at Fallon had been too poor for his first approach at the main runway so he'd tried to turn around and land on the other one. And that was where I had picked him up, whipping into that last desperate turn.

It baffled and angered me to think that for all the technology and all the knowledge and all the countless hours of studying and briefing and debriefing that went into these flights, and despite the fact that we were whole oceans away from where the real danger, the actual war, was taking place, something as simple as the weather, something as old and elemental as wind and ice, could still screw everything up and send a man into the ground. And ultimately there wasn't a single thing we could do about it.

That is either the most comforting or the most upsetting thing in the world and I still don't know which to call it.

The NTSB posts accident reports on its website, everything from aviation accidents to hazardous materials mishaps, vehicle crashes, marine accidents, and train wrecks. To a certain kind of person in a certain frame of mind, these reports can actually be deeply comforting. To me, the aviation reports are especially soothing because even though they are graphic encounters with seemingly infinite variations on my worst nightmare, their mechanical language and fanatical attention to dissecting every last possible detail, and then issuing a flurry of forcefully and specifically worded warnings and recommendations, has much the same effect as hearing those words sputtered back in the steam of a shower from a student pilot learning them by heart.

I realized that even if there were no bold declarations of warning or definitive statements coming from the crash I saw, I could still look back at the early days of Ross's journey through flight school and truly understand where all those other cautionary lessons keeping him safe came from and how expensive they were to learn, and from that I could extrapolate an intense feeling of gratitude and reverence for all the altered lives and stories beneath those terse, all-capped words.

Finally, seeing the crash was a jolting reminder that Ross and

I still had time. I was depressed and we were both exhausted, things between us were not good, but we were both still alive with one healthy son and another on the way. Sometimes it takes looking at the ultimate bottom line to realize that the place you happen to be stuck isn't nearly as bad as it seems.

CHAPTER 21

My reemergence from the fog of depression had taken nearly three months, a span of time I mourned for all the things I missed, and I found myself taking big greedy lungfuls of the scent of Sam's neck and hugging his squirming body around the bulk of my belly in an attempt to apologize for having faded through so much in our last weeks together before his brother arrived. For his part, the new baby, having loitered in his womb world a full four days past his due date, was like someone realizing he's going to be late to work, and he banged around grabbing his keys and gulping his breakfast and whatever else it is babies do on their way out. Meanwhile, I was determinedly lumbering around my kitchen with one earbud in, putting away dishes, making cookies, and stopping to bend over and breathe the word "choo" at the floor.

Childbirth the second time around was all about trying to incorporate the lessons Ross and I had learned in round one. There was a Plan, but it was merely a piece of paper with some words on it and I understood it as such. My mom had been summoned a full two weeks before the due date, and had thus already put a lot of effort into wrangling Sam and stocking the freezer, tasks that she continued as I sent Ross off to work to set his out-of-office message and tie up a few last details. My world, as the contractions got closer and stronger, shrank to a diameter of no more than five feet with a bright point of focus at the center. Everything else, including the question of whether or not I would get an epidural again this time, was pushed outside the circle.

If I thought I could handle it, and if it were not wholly against my nature, I might try this radical focus-limiting thing more often because the result was that everything I asked for unfolded before me with little or no resistance. I called Ross when I needed to go to the hospital and he was already on his way. When we reached the hospital, the nurse showed me how to hold Ross's hand by gripping his overlapped fingers instead of in a handshake grip, which meant I could clamp down as hard I needed to without grinding his knuckles or breaking his fingers. He was there beside me the whole time, answering the nurses' questions when I couldn't speak, helping untangle me from the various cords and monitors when I insisted on clawing my way out of the bed to pace and whimper, and repeating, "I'm here, I'm here, I'm so proud of you."

I had decided against pain medication again, but for totally different reasons. The preceding months had taught me that so many of the things I had taken for granted could be easily lost, despite the best efforts of everyone involved—jets could crash, a marriage could nearly unravel, and the treacherous currents of my depression could nearly tug me under. All of this could happen and the process hurt so badly that it didn't hurt at all. I was sick of being numb. But the persistent and inexorable force of a new life, and the privilege of bearing it, imperfect as I was—I wanted to feel every second of it.

Seven pounds, nine ounces, and twenty inches long, Wesley arrived on the same day that Venus briefly passed in front of the sun, the second in a pair of transits eight years apart and comprising one of the rarest of predictable astronomical phenomena. Eclipses, transits, and planetary orbits are not normally events I make note of. I had completely missed the first one in the pair, which had occurred roughly one month after Ross and I got engaged in 2004, but when I had a baby with the second one, I let my mind riff on the metaphorical implications of long but predictable separations, a planet named for the goddess of love, and the boldness of it crossing between our world and the sun as a tiny black dot I might have otherwise missed were I not looking at everything with wonder and amazement. With his arrival, I felt like I was finally getting a glimpse of the complexities of our family's orbits and the deep love that kept them spinning. Love and distance, it seemed, were the two biggest factors in learning how big my world could be, and that insight felt like a privilege I could only have earned in struggle and doubt, and in the pain of having almost lost it all.

Ross and I waded back into the fatigue and sleeplessness of parenting a newborn like walking into a freezing surf, but this time I made sure to stay on my antidepressant and to reflect often, and with gratitude, on the single biggest lesson I'd learned from Sam: babies are remarkably resilient, and I'd already made it through twenty months of raising one without accidentally killing him. We also had help again—my mom stayed on for the first week of Wes's life, and several of the wives signed up to bring us home-cooked dinners in the weeks immediately following the birth. To someone constantly preoccupied with the fear that her social awkwardness and imperfections, once discovered, will permanently exile her from the tribe, this simple act of kindness was stunning and humbling. I remember every single meal and was often struggling not to cry in accepting them. It's a kindness I now take every opportunity to pass on.

Months passed in a kind of cloistered, affectionate exhaustion. I counted the days successful if I could grab a fifteen-minute nap, and the weeks equally so if I managed to shower at least three times. Still, the exhaustion remained only that: exhaustion. I thought about deep, uninterrupted sleep with a covetousness that was outright lustful, but there were no dark, unshakable thoughts about my being an utter failure as a human being, no sudden flashes of rage, and no random bouts of weeping and self-maiming behind the furniture. I counted myself lucky and tried to become worthy of this relative clarity of mind by remembering to write down snippets of how our early days together unfolded, hoping that I could grab and record a few things to tell the boys when they were older.

Sam was a doting and carefully observant older brother. He practiced his own parenting skills on a stuffed doll he dragged around by the hair and called Baby, often sitting down cross-legged next to wherever I sat cradling Wes, and holding Baby up to his bared chest to nurse. He was wide-eyed and quiet through Wes's early crying spells and took to simultaneously embracing, bouncing, and patting a variety of toys, including plastic tractors and tiny animal figurines, while saying, "Oh, oh, oh . . . ssh, ssh . . . s'okay . . ." For such an intensely energetic toddler, this change was totally unexpected.

Parenting two kids close in age was a weird mental juggling act where I switched constantly between trying to remember all the old newborn routines and milestones while simultaneously trying to anticipate the entirely new terrain of toddlerhood. It felt like speaking two languages at once. I stumbled across a few moments that were so layered with meaning for me that it became difficult for me to separate out the objective experience of what happened from my own stunned emotional response. An example: When Sam first learned to say "I love you," he would say it only as he ran away, slammed a door, or hid his face behind a wall, a chair, or the opaque, pebbly glass of the shower stall. This was almost always accompanied by peals of laughter, and when I realized that he was using the words as a teasing substitute for "good-bye," and that he did this because it was always the last thing Ross said to him before he walked out the door for work, and the last thing I said before I walked out of his room at night, I was at first speechless and stunned. Then I resolved to smudge the association between "I love you" and absence by saying it all the damned time. Good morning, I love you! Here's a sandwich and I love you! I love you, and you should put that down!

Later, during a period in which Sam didn't see Ross for almost three weeks, two of those because Ross was on a basic fighter maneuvers detachment and one because after that he came home every evening long past Sam's bedtime and left again in the dark predawn hours before he woke up, Sam yelled at me suddenly from his car seat, "Want to moosh Daddy's flight suit! Want to *moosh* Daddy's pickup truck!" "Moosh" was the most violent word he knew at the time, aside from "bonk," and the flight suit and pickup truck were the two most tangible symbols of Ross and his absence. I didn't know how to respond to this one. I still vividly remembered how powerfully I loathed seeing my dad's olive green duffel bag laid out on the bed, ready to be packed, and how equally elated I was when I spotted it coming around the luggage carousel when we picked him up again at the airport. I think I ended up agreeing that the flight suit and pickup could probably do with a good mooshing.

Gratitude—for my healthy children, for every one of Ross's uneventful flights, for a relatively smooth patch of mental health despite the exhaustion—goes a long way, but almost immediately after Wes's birth, pressures at work picked up for Ross again and I found myself solo parenting a newborn and a twenty-one-month-old around the clock. Then we all started getting sick. A stunning variety of "bugs" ping-ponged back and forth between Ross and me and the boys, and all the fevers, the vomit, the sleepless nights, the random trips to the ER, just multiplied our workload. There was no relief. At work, Ross's colleagues started calling him "Patient Zero" and telling jokes about his two remaining white blood cells.

Around this time, Mikayla started traveling extensively for a nonprofit organization she had started. The best friend I had envisioned raising babies with was out of town most of the time, and it took me a while to realize that even when she was at home, she was less and less interested in hanging out with me. She was much more committed to her friendship with another one of the wives and, rather than taking this in stride, I fretted over what I'd done to offend her, tried and failed to win her back, and then spent great amounts of energy mourning our lost connection. If I hadn't been so busy moping about being what I called "friend dumped" and staring sadly at my back fence, I might have seen my brief, intense bond with Mikayla for what it was—an obvious attempt to find a bandage for the bleeding loss of Stella.

Distanced once again by our schedules, Ross and I fostered a perplexing silent competition over which of us was the most over-worked and amassed small armies of resentments, strategically deploying them in the few precious hours we had together. When we first moved to Fallon, I had seen TOPGUN as a rescue, a lucky twist of fate that kept Ross from going to Afghanistan for most of Sam's infancy, but now it seemed like the monumental stress and the brutal schedule of this three-year shore tour were creating a distance between us that may as well have been oceans. I was sick of feeling like my only option, always, was to acquiesce, to flex, to wait, to compromise—above everything else, I was learning, being a TOPGUN wife required patience, and I was nearing the end of mine.

We fought volcanically about an expensive camera I'd bought with award money from graduate school, and how I could never seem to remember to put it back in its case, and then about a mark I noticed on Sam's shoulder, the origins of which neither of us knew exactly, but that I feared could easily have appeared during one of Ross's intense, nearly nose-to-nose disciplining moments. It would have been easy to squeeze too hard—I knew this from nearly having done it myself—but I also knew I couldn't live with myself if I didn't bring it up. The resulting fight was one that left us both tearstained and utterly spent, him deeply wounded from an accusation he found unthinkable, and me openly unsure of whether I trusted him not to hurt our children. I felt bound—by babies, debt, illness, isolation, the daunting cost and logistics of travel, and law—to a man I hardly ever saw and then fought with when I did. The Singapore divorce talk was a joke compared to this, a tiny squall we sailed through relatively easily and counted ourselves seasoned.

Thus did we end up in marriage counseling a second time, but with a much better therapist, who let on that she saw many military couples and that our situation was neither unique nor unsalvageable. Ross also had the explicit support of his then skipper, a divorced father who encouraged Ross to do whatever it took to keep his family together. This made a huge difference in the attitudes both of us brought into counseling—his that marriage counseling was a legitimate use of an evening hour in which he could have been staying on at work, and mine that the Navy did actually give a shit if the job was eating people alive. Removing the scheduling and prioritization roadblocks allowed us to put Ross's job back into context, that is, as only one thing among many weighing on us and making demands on our collective resources.

We needed this steadying hand, this dedicated time solely for addressing the static between us. Ross explained his perspective on TOPGUN in a way that I could finally understand: "We do nothing but point out the flaws in everyone's execution of everything—even personal flaws. We do it much so that that's how you know you're accepted. That's the whole point—to get better." Articulated like that, with a fondness in his voice that I'll admit I found maddening, I could see it—to Ross, the time in Fallon was hard because it was important. He had been handed huge responsibilities and was expected to hew to an exacting standard. It was inevitable that some of that would come home.

I had something I needed to explain to Ross as well. What our time in Fallon meant to *me*, and what I realized only after battling my way through it, was that I no longer wanted to have divorce as my nuclear option. Admitting this to Ross—that I'd considered the idea, enough to have come up with the beginnings of a plan—was difficult for two reasons. First, he has always maintained that any talk of divorce has always been one-sided, that he has never and would never consider it an option. Talking openly of the possibility of leaving someone who claims that they would never leave you is difficult, even reviewing it in hindsight together. Second, and more pointedly, my taking divorce off the table directly affected the tone of the negotiation we needed to take up next.

Shore duty was coming to an end, and again, three possible duty stations lay before us—Lemoore, Virginia Beach, and Japan. We were assigned a billet back in Lemoore, and though I had initially been disappointed to miss out on Virginia Beach a second time, I was ecstatic about reuniting with Stella and Jake. The next two years would have us on the hook for possible deployments; but more important, we faced a final decision about whether or not we would take a substantial Department Head retention bonus and recommit to the Navy. By saying I wouldn't divorce him, I was in one way weakening my hand, but ironically, declaring that intention was the wall I needed at my back to dig in and fight to keep us all together while fortifying and defending my own boundaries.

CHAPTER 22

A month before we moved back to Lemoore, Ross's father died. My parents came out to take care of Sam and Wes, and Ross and I flew back to Texas for the funeral. In his crisp, perfect whites, Ross spoke beautifully and candidly to the gathering of friends and family about his father, stood tall and quiet with his brother and his mother in the pews, and bowed his head at the graveside after his father was laid to rest. If there was an unexpected breakdown happening, it was mine. I sniffled through our plane ride, wept openly through the entire funeral service, and was unable to say even one cogent thing to any of the assembled mourners. People who had known and loved Danny for decades before I met him were comforting *me*, and this only made me cry harder.

I would have been hard-pressed to explain it at the time, but partly I was mourning the father I had seen in Ross long before we'd ever had kids, back when we were dating. I've heard men joke that a good way to see how a potential wife will age is to look at her mother. I don't think it's a stretch to say that women could learn a good deal about a potential husband by looking at his father. Danny had a warm, easygoing nature and he shared a deep connection with Ross, and he'd passed on a vast body of knowledge—a knack for all things mechanical, a passion for camping and hiking, an appreciation of slapstick and Peter Sellers movies, and a love of classic country music. In him, I saw someone who had poured his heart into being a father.

While these impressions were accurate, they were also things I learned about Danny at a time in his life when the acceleration of his disease meant he wasn't working anymore, that he was home and emotionally present and willing to talk about his best memories in a way that's probably only possible when you know you'll soon be forgetting almost all of it. I never knew him in the years he was focused on earning a living as a soil scientist and working at various national laboratories and research firms. It's quite possible that he was just as focused on his work as my own father, whom I've subjected to much closer, harsher scrutiny. I loved Danny because he was a wonderful man, but also because he was a prism who refracted for me the most beautiful image of fatherhood, all of the beauty I had known and none of the warts. At his funeral I cried for all the things that still stood in the way of Ross and me being our best selves as parents. I cried for the time we'd lost fighting, for the doubts I'd harbored, and for the good man I still loved hopelessly. And lastly, I cried for the way ahead, where I still couldn't see how we would make room for our family on a military calendar.

By the time we returned to Nevada, I felt like I had no tears left, which was a relief because there was a lot to do. A nurse at the base clinic had accidentally perforated Sam's eardrum on one of our many sick calls a few months prior, and the specialist we'd been sent to in Reno had recommended that as soon as it healed, his tonsils, constantly swollen and now almost to the point of touching, be removed. The tonsillectomy would happen ten days before our move, which meant packing up the house with one toddler on pain meds and the other running under foot. But even this was not enough to dampen my spirits about closing the Fallon chapter of our lives.

Awaiting us on base in Lemoore was the exact same house we had lived in before on Hellcat Court. This kind of coincidence is almost unheard of in the high-turnover world of base housing, and though we had other options to choose from, something about returning to a place we knew appealed to us both. Moving back into the same house meant I got to feel things I hadn't felt for decades, like a sense of history, of returning to roots already planted, even if shallowly. It also meant I got an exact physical measure of how drastically our lives had changed in three short years by measuring how differently we fit into the same space. *I remember when we didn't know what to do with this room. I remember when I crawled down this hall in labor. I remember cutting myself over in that corner and sitting by that window at four a.m. with a wide-awake baby convinced I would never feel any better. I remember before that, sitting in the exact same place and wishing we could have children, wondering if we ever would . . .*

And now here we were with no spare bedrooms in which to hide from each other, and so much noise. There were no hazy areas where we just stashed stuff we wanted to forget about, boxes we didn't want to unpack; every square inch had to be accounted for. But before we unpacked anything, Ross took three days and a whole lot of paint and transformed the white walls into the palate of soft grays we'd chosen. A few months later, for Mother's Day, he surprised me by doing the kitchen too, and choosing a warm, vibrant yellow-green called Wheatgrass. I loved it.

It was ironic, but this all-purpose reusable house that we would definitely leave again felt more mine, more like home, than anywhere I'd lived since I was thirteen years old. And it had nothing to do with the house itself and everything to do with how we filled it, how we'd grown, and who we'd become.

We weren't the only ones who had changed. Stella and Jake immediately welcomed us into their home, and I marveled at the tall, sun-browned girl and boy who had replaced the giggling toddlers who had toppled all the houseplants one day when their dad was deployed. I had hoped we could all just pick up where we left off, but life is more complicated than that. In the three years we'd been gone, Stella and Jake had become close with another couple whose kids were closer in age to their own. This new couple came up often in conversation—the family trips they took together, the jokes and stories they shared. I was jealous, but I had also learned that you can't force relationships, both friendships and marriages, to conform to your own hopeful fantasies.

As spring moved into summer, Ross and I began spending more time with another couple a few blocks away on base. Aaron and Elizabeth were newly married, and Ross had known and liked Aaron from previous squadrons where they had worked together. They both shared a love of craft beer and ridiculous costume parties. When I met Elizabeth, a psychologist from Boston who was just as irreverent as Aaron and also fearlessly emotional and honest, we finally had another four-way friendship match. Aaron and Elizabeth were just at the beginning of their road to starting a family, and as I set things aside—Wes's newly outgrown crib, baby blankets, sheets, clothes, and toys—I thought gratefully of Stella and Jake and this chance to pass on the favor. I fell with gratitude and abandon into a deep friendship with Elizabeth, even though we both knew that by the time she would be a new mother and most in need of someone to lean on, I would be preparing to relocate.

The decision about whether or not to take the bonus was a hard one to make, and Ross and I took as long as we possibly could with it. Saying yes would commit us to another four years, at which point Ross would have accrued fourteen years of service, just six shy of the magic vesting point of twenty years, when the government promises a pension and continued health care. We spent months piling up facts and asking questions. Who's gotten out and where did they find a job? Who's staying in and are they happy? I nearly went cross-eyed poring over an Excel spreadsheet Ross had created that laid out his entire career thus far and possible forks in the road ahead. Evaluation periods, possible raises and promotions, chunks of years with deployments and chunks without, moves and potential destinations—they were all laid out, beautifully color coded, along a timeline showing Ross's age, potential rank, and salary, all the way up to the twenty-year mark. Beneath this line, I sketched in the ghost script of my own age and the ages of our boys, when elementary school started, when I'd like to go back to work, when they hit the rapids of junior high and high school, and where we might be when they got ready to leave us. I stared at all of these intersecting and overlapping lines, trying to see the various futures they laid out. I knew Ross was well positioned for a successful active-duty career if that was what we chose, but I also couldn't see any way out of him missing large chunks of the boys' lives.

One mid-September evening when Ross and I were still weighing our decision, I gazed idly out my kitchen window while finishing up the supper dishes and watched as Connor and Emma, neighbor kids two and five years old, trotted out in their pj's to check the mail. On that particular day, their mom, a new friend of mine, had woken to the news that her husband's squadron, en route to its destination for a ten-month combat deployment and conducting a training exercise, had lost a jet, one of two that went down in the Pacific after a midair collision. One pilot, the one from her squadron and not, thank God, her husband, had ejected and been recovered. He was in fair condition. The other pilot was still missing, later to be confirmed dead.

I stood in front of my kitchen window and watched as the sun caught their hair, and I thought, "Their dad is okay, thank God for that," but it was like I had watched a target level over these two little kids, playmates of my own children, and then move on. There were roughly fifteen pilots in their dad's squadron, and training flights like the one that had gone wrong that day launched all the time. I'd spent the morning in the Starbucks on base trying to write, only to abandon the effort after eavesdropping on the conversation of some nearby wives and, embarrassed but unable to stop myself, intruding with, "Wait, I'm sorry—did you say there's been a crash? Do you know which squadron?"

It feels like an X-ray, this thing that passes over us all when the news of a crash starts to spread. A friend I passed on my way out of the coffee shop just stopped me without a word and gave me a hug. This is when all the walls in our community come down, when everyone looks each other in the eye and doesn't have to say a thing. I had no idea what I would say to my friend as I threw my stuff into the front seat of my car and headed to her house—I just knew I had to see her. I wonder about the effect of this beam of awareness coming over us, testing the soundness of our bones, our organs, the heart of our faith. Is it damaging us, this radiationlike scrutiny and awareness of our own mortality? Or are we more alive to the reality of the world than our more insulated civilian counterparts?

It was at moments like this one, standing at the kitchen sink and feeling a sudden and crushing tenderness for someone else's kids who had no idea what just narrowly passed them by, that I felt a confused sort of rage, a wave of heat and electricity that told me I had found one of my boundaries.

CHAPTER 23

Over the course of many long, difficult conversations in the following months about whether or not to take the bonus, Ross and I hammered out our "hard noes," points in the negotiation on which each of us was unwilling to compromise.

"I'm open to changing the job," Ross said, "but not the business of tactical flight. I don't want to fly commercial airliners—I can't be a bus driver. And I think a desk job might kill me."

"I can't do the deployments," I said. "Ten months plus all the work-ups beforehand? That's more than a year of the boys' lives you'd be missing. You can't get that back."

Just when it seemed we were deadlocked, we discovered a third option, one that initially looked like it was closed to us: full-time support, or FTS, in the Navy Reserve. The Reserve exists, ostensibly, to support and augment the active-duty community in terms of "troop readiness," but in reality the two are funded and run very differently. The transition from active duty to FTS is not one that's heavily advertised or promoted, and it involves a terrifying leap over the chasm of unemployment because you have to completely resign from one community to even apply to the other.

For us, FTS could look like this: Ross could train F/A-18 squadrons by flying as their "red air," or pretend enemy, in a dedicated adversary squadron. We could start out in one of four locations—Fallon, Virginia Beach, Key West, or New Orleans. He'd have a similar salary and continue to make rank and work toward his pension, but he *would not deploy*. It seemed like such a perfect compromise for us, honoring both the love of flying jets and the desire for a more stable home life. I wanted to leave it that way and focus on the next hurdle, the application period and hoping we could avoid a gap between the time Ross was honorably discharged from active duty and the time he started flying again with FTS. I think Ross wanted this too, but again, life is more complicated than that.

Given his preference of flying real estate, Ross would put Fallon as his first choice. The desert canyons, the salt flats, the mountains—all of it makes for some thrilling flying. But I can't see myself going back. A house there legally belongs to us, the only place in the world that does, and when I imagine crossing its threshold again, or facing myself in its bathroom mirrors, when I imagine parking my car under those garage door tracks every day and lifting my kids out beneath them, I get a knot in my stomach.

For his part, Ross clearly has his reservations about giving up active duty. Coming back from a brief boat detachment to keep his carrier landing qualifications current, Ross said, "God, I'm going to miss it. That feeling when you first launch out? There's nothing like it. I was up there above the water and looking down on the boat . . . It's all I've ever wanted." He looked straight at me and shook his head, saying it again: "It's all I've ever wanted."

I nodded and gave him a sad smile, but it stung, standing there in front of him in the kitchen with our sons giggling and making faces at each other over the breakfast table behind us. *Really? That's* all *you've ever wanted? All I've ever wanted is right here in this room.* But I didn't say it. I told myself that was not what he meant. "He'll need to grieve," his mother told me later over the phone, and I hung on to this as my shield, knowing I might need to raise it again. The occasion presented itself one night as we were remembering the days of flight school. We were laughing together about the miserable and aggressive Dobermans who had lived on the other side of the chain-link fence in our backyard, and how I'd lost my temper with them one day and unwittingly stumbled on the way to win them over: spraying them in their faces with my garden hose. "You would have been so much happier as a helo wife," he said, without a trace of malice. He meant it as an apology for the desolate places we'd lived, but I also couldn't help seeing the wistful flash of an Alternate Ross, one who hadn't asked me to come with him when he went to OCS.

Even more complicated are the ways our boys weigh in without even meaning to. Sam has grown into a blond, fair-skinned version of his father, and one of his favorite pastimes is cobbling together imitation flight gear—a bicycle helmet, swim goggles, and a surgical mask with an orange accordion tube sticking out of it doubled as a flight helmet and breathing mask for a long time. At his recent preschool graduation, Sam's answer to what he wanted to be when he grew up was, "A pilot just like my dad." His questions about everything seem to have no end, and recently he's begun to ask about wars, about the gates we drive through every day, about the armed guards who check my ID. One night he asked, "Will they shoot me if I don't eat my broccoli?" Horrified,

I told him no, never, and thereafter encouraged him to unroll his window as we passed through and wave at the guards. He looks forward to it now and often shouts some random question to them as we pull up.

One of Wes's first words was "jet!" shouted anytime one streaked overhead. He has one go-to demand right before heading into a two-year-old's meltdown, and he deploys it only when he knows I can't deliver: "I want Daddy!"

I can see what I'm fighting for—a safe place to raise our sons, a life that makes more room for our family than the one we're currently living, a family without whole years completely dad-less. I can also see what Ross is fighting for—lasting membership in a unique (if nomadic) community, a pension that could start in as little as a decade, but mostly the chance to live out a dream.

Where we are now is a place we're familiar with: living, for at least twelve more months, in a house we'll never see again once we leave it and poised to move to one of four cities in four different corners of the country if Ross's application to FTS is accepted. The unfamiliar part, the part that scares us so much we barely talk about it, is the possibility, however slim, that our change of course might not work out, that when the time comes to leave the Navy, that other trapeze bar may elude our grasp and we may have to reinvent ourselves entirely. Either way, the delicate balance of power within our marriage is bound to keep shifting back and forth in the years ahead.

We are two people who love each other very much and who want the best for the beautiful sons we've brought into the world. The past ten years have changed us into older, harder, warier versions of our younger selves, but we've held true to our dreams, and to each other, even though sometimes that same holding on has cost us both dearly. Some days we're allies fighting for a joint cause; some days we square off against each other. But through it all we've learned strategies, coping mechanisms, tactics—some of the successful ones passed down from our parents and some of the unsuccessful ones too. *That's the whole point—to get better.* Neither of us has ever crossed into a combat zone, but there have been casualties, and ours is most definitely a war. Some things are worth fighting for.

ACKNOWLEDGMENTS

My mom was my first and best reader, and my U.N. airlift for childcare, emotional support, and freezable meals in times of disaster. My dad is and always has been my biggest fan, even when it meant being my punching bag. My brother, an extraordinary writer himself, was both a memory bank and a tune-up mechanic on my sense of humor. Thank you.

Profound thanks to my extraordinary agent, Kristyn Keene at ICM, who believed in this book when it was still years from being finished, and whose gentle encouragement kept me from giving up. Thank you also to Sloan Harris. Sarah Stein, my editor at Penguin, has incredible instincts and I feel lucky to have worked with her. Thanks also to Sheila Moody, Min Lee, Roseanne Serra, Shannon Kelly, Carlynn Chironna, and all the folks at Penguin.

I am so fortunate to have had excellent teachers and mentors over the years. Most recently, Steve Yarbrough took a chance on me and opened a door I wouldn't have thought to knock on. Steven Church inspired and encouraged me and was a great friend. My gratitude as well to John and Connie Hales, Tanya Nichols, David Shields, John Trimble, Mia Carter, Laura Furman, and, way back in the ninth grade in Saudi Arabia, David Jackson: all helped me find my voice.

I would be a much weaker writer were it not for the MFA Program at California State University, Fresno and the many talented writers who welcomed me into their community, offering feedback and friendship. The Bread Loaf Writers' Conference was where I first started to see this knot of essays as a book, and where I was lucky enough to meet Mary Westbrook, Rolf Yngve, Sonia Hsieh, Nora Costello, Jeff Stauch, Megan Griswold, Elena Passarello, and Alexandria Marzano-Lesnevich, inspirations all. Thanks to the CSU Summer Arts program and the funding support of the Division of Graduate Studies. Thank you also to the *Colorado Review, Front Porch Journal*, and *The Atlantic* for publishing or recognizing early essay versions of some of these chapters.

For their generous early reads, thank you to Siobhan Fallon, Karl Marlantes, Steve Yarbrough, Katey Schultz, Anthony Swofford, Steven Church, and Alison Buckholtz.

I am grateful for my Navy family, though it is too large to name individually. A few to whom I owe a special debt: Heidi and Ben Charles, Mary and Wes Kennerly, Dynelle and Isaac Long, Kristen and Tony Roy, Kevin McLaughlin, Jennifer Reynolds, the staff and families of TOPGUN, and all of the members of the super exclusive Fallon book club. For their expertise, thank you to Cade Hines and Alex Wann. To every Navy wife who has shared her friendship with me, no matter how briefly: thank you. It's been more important than you know.

For their friendship and support, and for visiting me in various tiny military towns, thank you to Antoinette Curl, Kandra Rivers, and Larry Ballay.

I am indebted to the bravery and generosity of my in-laws,

Ruth and Danny Jackson. Special thanks as well to my grandparents, Rosa and Bill Starnes and Mary and Ray Martin, and to the aunts and uncles who have inspired me and shared their stories with me over the years. Uncle Dan, thank you for putting up with me as teenager. I hope I haven't embarrassed or shocked any of you too much.

And finally, for sharing his life with me through thick and thin, and for helping to create and support our beautiful family, thank you to my husband, Ross.